Bowler's Turn

BOWLER'S TURN

A FURTHER RAMBLE
ROUND THE REALM OF CRICKET

IAN PEEBLES

Introduction by Frank Keating

THE PAVILION LIBRARY

First published in Great Britain 1960

Copyright © I. A. R. Peebles 1960
Introduction copyright © Frank Keating 1987

First published in the Pavilion Library in 1987 by
Pavilion Books Limited
196 Shaftesbury Avenue, London WC2H 8JL
in association with Michael Joseph Limited
27 Wrights Lane, Kensington, London W8 5TZ

Consulting Editor: Steve Dobell

British Library Cataloguing in Publication Data
Peebles, Ian
Bowler's turn.
1. Cricket
I. Title
796.35'8   GV917

ISBN 1-85145-145-5
ISBN 1-85145-118-8 Pbk

Printed and bound in Great Britain by
Billing & Sons Limited, Worcester

INTRODUCTION

I had heard of Ian Peebles, of course. Even to a short-trousered, urchin sports-nut in the wartime West of England, the name made for a good quiz question: Name Scotland's English leg-spinner who had diddled out the Don a decade before? I suppose I must have read him too, in the *Sunday Graphic* or *Everybody's*, though at the time the erudite sparkle was lost on an oik who, at that age, was voracious only for the facts and figures of the Gloucestershire scorecard in our local *Citizen*. I must have been in the same room as Ian for the first time that midsummer Saturday in the early 1960s when, as sporting dogsbody for the *Slough Observer*, I conned a pass for a day to the sanctum of the Lord's press box. Here were the giants of this tyro's trade. I quaked as they eyed me with haughty disdain: golly, they all used fountain pens, and flashy cigarette holders, and drank *wine*. And never seemed to be watching the cricket! I was convinced I would never make the grade. Ian was then on the *Sunday Times* — and was to relate years later:

'There were rivalries, feuds, enmities, and prejudices . . . the few notorious dislikes belonging among people in the same newspaper group. For my part, I look back on much help and co-operation, and a great deal of good company and interesting talk. Fun and jest from the astringent wit of Jim Kilburn to Clive Taylor's amusing drolleries. The *Times* crossword was a great solace, and Kilburn, Bill Bowes and John Solon were each and collectively shrewd performers. The nice acid tang in Alex Bannister's quips was accentuated by a gravelly drawl. Asked about the health of a colleague, whom the enquirer knew he cordially disliked, he replied, "All right, I believe — between fits".'

I never knew that generation. By the time I was revelling in a brief run on the cricket writers' circuit, towards the end of the 1970s, those urbane and leisurely reporters had long clipped-in their fountain pens for the last time, and the game (with a few outstanding exceptions) was being covered by real Fleet Street pros, with biros and a relish for gossip columning, if not downright crime-writing. They still didn't watch the cricket, but now they weren't even bothering with the *Sun* crossword.

It was in that company, however, that I met Ian for the first time – as colleagues and soul-mates, too, for in his late 60s he began to contribute an occasional series of quite scintillating essays for my paper, *The Guardian*. We would meet at Lord's and he would hand in his copy to be passed on to the sports editor – and then take me to lunch, me purring with delight at his soft-told tales of wine, wickets, and song. He was pretty good on women, too! He taught me (without the slightest pretension) a little more each time about wine, and in return, at every lunch, I would insist he told me how he got Bradman at Old Trafford: '... when he had made 14, he again came down the wicket and played the same off-drive, only to snick the ball to second-slip, where Duleep made no mistake. A roar went up from the crowd that must have lasted a full minute and, for the moment, I had fulfilled my purpose. A well-known artist named Nevinson wrote later, in a book entitled *These Savage Islands*, that he had returned to these shores in the midst of a bank crisis, and various other disasters, to find, much to his disgust, that all the evening newspaper headlines said simply PEEBLES DOES IT.'

Ian being a son of the Manse, and me a Catholic, each time over our final one-for-the-stroll back to the office, I demanded to hear the classic of many *faux pas* by Lord Lionel Tennyson, with whom Ian had toured India in 1937. On board ship, his Lordship had made great friends of the then Prime Minister of Australia, Joe Lyons, a devout Catholic and proud father of a large family. 'They got along splendidly and whenever there was a pause in the conversation, Lionel was ready to fill it.

'"You've a lot of Catholics in Australia," he said.

'"Yes, indeed," replied Mr Lyons, with pardonable pride,

'about a third of the population.'

'"You want to watch 'em," cautioned Lionel. "You can't trust 'em – and what's more, the buggers breed like rabbits!"'

Happy days. In the winter of 1979–80, I was sent with Brearley's men to cover my first Australian tour. It was a thrilling experience – richly enhanced by a series of letters received, almost weekly it seemed, from Ian. I knew he was ill but had no inkling of it from the fizz and chuckle and exhortation contained in those regular signals on air-mail flimsy. I stayed at Melbourne's Windsor Hotel, mellow, brown-stained old relic from Ian's own touring days, years before. This delighted him. 'Make sure you walk to the ground every morning,' he insisted, 'through the park with its trees and grasses, and exquisite masses of flowers and colour.' Or, 'Get yourself a haircut, and go to Mr Brown's establishment and see if, behind the barber's chair, he still has the framed picture of Sammy Carter catching Jack Hobbs behind the wicket in 1921, a very notable catch.' Or, 'Remember in Australia that all cricket grounds are Ovals, and are tended not by groundsmen but by curators. Wonderful cricket grounds they are too.' The same warm flavours that permeate the beguiling *Bowler's Turn* that I now have in front of me.

When young Graham Gooch was run out for 99 in the Melbourne Test, almost by return came a four-page letter-essay on 'Great Knocks of 99', which was worthy of any all-time anthology (as long as the cavalier spelling was checked: as his friend, Mr Swanton, said in his introduction to a reissue of *Batter's Castle*, Ian had a 'positively mediaeval indifference to spelling'); and then, by next post, another engaging reflection on running between the wickets at Melbourne in the 1937 Test, when Ian's fondly remembered and scatty Middlesex comrade, Walter Robins, had come in to bat on the fifth evening, with 534 runs still needed and four wickets down. Maurice Leyland was still there, having battled his way through an intensely hot day against a spirited attack:

'It was with great relief (having scored nought in the first innings) that Walter steered O'Reilly's first ball through the gully and was off like a whippet from the trap. He was back for the second in a flash and, seeing no fielder in the vicinity of the ball, set off for a third. Halfway there he was aware of a figure by his side. It was Maurice, whom he had lapped. At once Walter turned back; Maurice plodded on to safety where, in a cloud of steam and sweat, he literally "sat on the splice", blowing like anything. As Walter advanced to make his apologies, Maurice tottered out to meet him. "Take it easy, lad," he gasped, "we can't get all these roody roons tonight."

PS: Keep up good work: I have a very drinkable *Côtes du Roussillon* for you when you return.

England's cricketers and their caravan of hangers-on returned from that tour to Heathrow airport on 21 February. I went home to the West Country for a few days' R & R before looking forward, amongst other things, to returning to London and splicing the bottle with Ian. Such tales to tell him. Within a week, on 29 February, the newspapers said he was dead. He was aged 72.

All his gusto and civilisation, generous love of life, and genial modesty are displayed in this reissue. It is still with sadness, but also a privileged one, that I warmly commend these contents to you.

Frank Keating

London, 1987

BOWLER'S TURN

A further ramble round the realm

of cricket

By IAN PEEBLES

Foreword by the Rt. Hon. R. G. Menzies
C.H., Q.C., M.P.

CONTENTS

BOWLER'S TURN

WITH THE M.C.C. IN THE WEST INDIES

Foreword

There is a great bond between those who love cricket. I sometimes wonder whether my electors feel that I devote an unfair proportion of my time to enjoying this wonderful game. Alas, I see it no more than a few days in each year, but in those few days I add to my "inner reserves" of happy recollections.

The game itself is, of course, a great art, and its great players great artists. There is no other game quite like it. Its subtleties may occasionally be "caviare to the general". In a duel between bowler and batsman, provided that they are both skilled, there is finesse, cunning, a quick and perceptive intelligence, and wit. You may query "wit", but I repeat it. For wit represents the quick pouncing of the mind, and the great cricketers know it.

Ian Peebles was a fine slow bowler, one of a class of men trained in art and patience, the fly fishermen of cricket. His playing time passed, and he became a writer. Not, thank heaven, one of those snappers-up of unconsidered trifles who prefer gossip to description and who are indifferent to the great contest going on at the wickets, but a true writer. He has an affection for the game, a respect for those who play it, and a scholar's command of English, for which he also has affection and respect.

Over many years now, he has given me singular pleasure. I am glad to know that once more that pleasure will be shared by thousands of others.

Canberra,
9th February, 1960.

R. G. MENZIES.

Opening Spell

CHAPTER ONE

Arranging the Field

LAST SEASON I WROTE SOME RATHER abridged reminiscences of cricket in the 'thirties for the *Sunday Times*, and was much warmed by the interest they aroused in the minds of several generations. It was plainly the period which stimulated this interest, irrespective of any merit or otherwise in the writings, whatever the wishful imaginings of the author. But it gave one to think.

The twenty years of cricket between the wars was, especially in the second decade, a unique age in the long history of cricket. It was rich in talent and spacious in setting despite the ever darkening background. When the clouds eventually burst it was an abrupt and complete end which overnight turned this live and gracious world of its own into a long-bygone memory. The changes to be wrought by the following six years were, as in the case of almost all things, to be deeper and greater than those caused by the previous upheaval.

For many who played it was clearly the end of their active days; for the aged it was the end of everything; for the young it was an incalculable rift, and for everyone the future was unpredictable but probably bleak. All this went to breed an intense nostalgia, so that the memories of the pre-war years were treasured with a jealous warmth which manifested itself in various forms, according to the circumstances of the individual.

When Service matches were started, people flocked to the grounds despite the expectation of an occasional delivery from Herr Hitler in the shape of a bomb or land mine.

BOWLER'S TURN

In the Services the troops and matelots did their best with such makeshift gear as they could find. I still recall my own efforts for our Field Regiment, stationed in Norfolk, which were probably typical of hundreds of others but which brought to light an East Anglian trait more usually (and often erroneously) attributed to Easterners a lot further to the North. The local squire lent us a field on condition that we mended his fences. A dear old lady loaned her mowing-machine—provided we weeded her drive. A farmer lent us his water-cart after we had pulled his thistles. The driver of a diesel roller was a reasonable bet at a couple of pints, and next day the County steam roller was pressed into service at the same price per head of crew. No-one rushed forward to aid the good old troops without thought of reward but, if they had any insight into our then state of efficiency, the helpers were perhaps justified in their outlook. Anyway, as things turned out, the Army once again had the last laugh. The day dawned when we were all set to enjoy the very creditable fruits of our labours and, by way of a prelude, the umpire bellowed a martial " play ". At that moment an emissary arrived to inform us that we were moving immediately to another location. Our umpire, still virginal in shining denim, then applied the closure with a few rather different but equally well chosen words, and a commendably bad grace.

But cricket as a going concern was rightly a very small diversion in the midst of tremendous and tragic events. In the minds of cricket devotees, however, the joy of those glorious days so recent and yet so finally and irrevocably gone became a precious and vivid compartment in the mind, for the most patriotic and energetic citizen had to have his moments of reflection on good times and things, if only to remind himself of the precious heritage for which he strove. So the cricket of the 'thirties had and still has a very special place in many hearts. It has also an immediate appeal to the modern generation as the last phase of an ancient era separated from them by an immeasurable gulf. They are, on the whole, wonderfully polite and attentive to its survivors and their reminiscences, if occasionally they find it difficult to suppress an indulgent smile.

If the tween-war years inspire a particular affection in a certain age group, it does not mean that any period is without charm to the lover of the game. But his regard for the great deeds of the past must be tempered by his age, experience and wisdom. When, forty years ago, I would pause, after the exhaustion of playing a Test Match series on the lawn against my brother, to pore over *The Jubilee Book of Cricket* I was delighted and impressed. I found it hard, however, to believe that the giants of that age could possibly pit their prehistoric technique against the mysteries of swerve and googly as practised by the reigning heroes. The constant castigation of their contemporary cricket by critics, who proclaimed the superiority of the old days, I ascribed to blind prejudice, and here I was probably not so far from the truth. It is only on discussing cricket matters with my son, now at the age where I was these forty years ago, that I have been bounced into making certain alarming mathematical calculations. In relative terms of time, the shadowy ancients who peered out of the *Jubilee Book* at me are, to him, the cricketers of the mid-thirties. It is, on the whole, gratifying that he is so indulgent, for he must be prey to the same doubts from which I suffered.

Not until the years of full maturity does one come to realise that cricket is a continuous and overlapping process and that evolution is gradual, indeed very gradual. Only the unthinking denigrates his cricket forebears and, in like pattern, stubbornly refuses to recognise his successors. Technique must advance and the general standard must improve as the number of active participants increases, although this does not mean that there are not lean periods of execution for various material reasons. It is a fair assumption that the champions of one era would, with very little adjustment, be leaders of the next if, to sustain my argument at the risk of some complication, they could not be expected to excel the established best. I had a fair indication of this probability when, at a very early age, I shared a net with Plum Warner and G. A. Faulkner, both then in retirement for some years past. I can't recall at this advanced stage, seeing the leg break and googly better spun, or a batsman who combined soundness and polish in a greater degree. I believe without reservation that Sydney Barnes was the greatest bowler of all time. And, to keep the record in balance, Godfrey Evans had moments beyond any other wicket-keeper within my ken, while Ray Lindwall had the most comprehensive armament of the pacemen.

My case, then, is that the intelligent student sees each age in its proper perspective and not through blinkers of the damping "In my day" pattern. That is not to say that the observer should condone ill trends and tendencies which periodically arise, but, to be constructive, he must seek the cause, and not merely dismiss them as the inevitable folly of an age to which he does not belong. "Body-line" bowling was a passing excrescence which arose out of a frustrating domination of bat (principally wielded by Bradman) over ball. English cricket underwent two conspicuously lean post-war periods, for obvious reasons. There have been cults of negative bowling and tactics, and here the causes are less perceptible and more complex. I have, very reluctantly, come to believe that the alteration to the LBW law has contributed to these ills, but still recognise the injustice of the previous ruling. Bad wickets over a period have had a disastrous effect on English cricket, but happily the elements responsible for them, namely ground authorities and the weather, seem to have had a change of heart. One season of sunshine and true pitches has already had a most salutary effect. Indeed as I write the facts of the situation and the portents lead one to believe that we could be on the threshold of an era in which efficiency could well be allied to real entertainment, for the apparent advance in England is well matched by the renaissance in Australia, where there is a fine modern school of batsmen led by O'Neill. There are also some splendid young bowlers to be seen down under, but the widespread evil of throwing will have to be extirpated before the orthodox plant can come to full flower.

In writing this book I have therefore pursued a loose pattern of the three ages of cricket that I have known, and to expand the views I have so far briefly expressed. It is again a collection of reminiscences, impressions and ideas, and I say a loose pattern as it has not always been possible to fit things into exact chronological order.

I have also included another couple of purely fictional tales as quite a few readers of *Batter's Castle* were kind enough to ask for more. Some also asked whom I had in mind when I said they were inspired by a very old and now departed friend. Although the characters answer to the time-honoured formula regarding "no living persons . . . etc." there is no harm in saying that the central character might bear some resemblance to Dick Burrows who played for Worcestershire and whom I knew later as umpire and scorer. With his cheerfulness, humour, real goodness of heart and manners he earned, and could well have inspired, that hard worked title "nature's gentleman."

Of the ages I have known, the present is undoubtedly the widest in interest, active and academic. More people play cricket in the world than ever before, more people read about it and a huge public listen to radio comments and watch it on television. That gates for first class matches have fallen both in this country and Australia is only indicative of the immense amount of counter attraction made available by the improvement of transport facilities, headed by the family motor car. There are other factors in a much changed world which contribute to the conclusion that, although the public watches less, the interest has not waned and its field is enormously widened.

There have always been Jeremiahs who have clearly observed the signs of the decline and eventual, indeed imminent, decease of the cricket body corporate. They have always been wrong and in all probability will always be. There have, as I have said, been passing malaises which

17

BOWLER'S TURN

have bored and irritated the faithful, but the point is they have passed. When they reappear in different form they will once again pass. Cricket will doubtless change in some respects, especially in the case of six day county cricket and, when supersonic aircraft set one down at the pavilion door, annual internationals may take the place of prolonged tours. But the game itself will remain fundamentally unchanged and will live as long as man is born in his present form.

CHAPTER TWO

The Roaring Twenties

I WAS TEN AND A HALF YEARS OLD WHEN
the first war ended and not surprisingly had never seen
a cricket match. Not surprisingly because not only was
there little cricket to be seen in Scotland at that period,
but our war time home was Wick, eighteen miles south
of John o'Groats where little organised cricket has ever
been seen. My father being discharged shortly before the
actual end of the hostilities, we moved to Uddingston, a
village near—now a suburb of—Glasgow. The following
year the local cricket club re-opened, and with it a new
world for me.

Not long after my initiation my father, who was a very
good club cricketer, took me to the ground of the Poloc
Club in Glasgow where the Australian Imperial Forces
were playing a Scottish XI. This was a somewhat disillu-
sioning experience for me, as the Australians thrashed the
local bowling to over seven hundred for six wickets at an
average rate of over two runs a minute. Four of them
made hundreds, and one, Jack Murray, whom I met in
Adelaide almost forty years later, made a hundred and
fifty. He broke four bats in the process, and continually
struck the ball into or over the tops of the surrounding
trees. At each of these gigantic wafts my father's face
would light up with a smile of incredulous delight and
he would cry "Well away, Sir—oh well away." My own
feelings were rather of grudging astonishment and when
Cyril Docker, another friend of later years, overwhelmed
the home side for 85 and 88 I could only suppose that the
Scottish hand was better suited to the basket hilted sword
than the bat handle. Stirred by these unhappy doubts I
asked my father whether English cricket was better than

Scottish cricket, at which he laughed and said "Considerably". It seemed to me at the age of eleven to be a bitter injustice that the only English institution which could possibly excel its Scottish equivalent should be the one that I loved best. However, love, as ever, conquered all and my brother and I became profound experts on every phase of the county championship. When England set sail to meet Australia our loyalty was at fever heat. To this day I can remember gulping in the views of a correspondent to a popular newspaper who extolled the irresistible all-round powers of our team. "There will be Hobbs crashing the ball through the covers, while sturdy Jack Russell attends to the on-side . . . Parkin's funny stuff will baffle the uninitiated—lots of batting—bags of bowling".

When England had lost all 5 test matches with ease, disillusionment was terrible indeed. Nothing so appalling had happened since Joe Beckett, on his triumphant road to the world heavy-weight championship, had been smacked flat in seventy seconds by a Frenchman with a name quite different from the way it was spelt. Had our cricketers been chloroformed or hypnotised by the opposing manager as we knew Beckett had been? (I had not then experienced Manager Sydney Smith's oratorical powers which, though painstaking, discount any element of spell-binding.) There must have been some explanation and I wondered what my correspondent thought about it. No doubt he gave it the full "glaring shortcomings as foretold in this newspaper" treatment, but by that time he had lost one reader for good and all.

Hope was by no means dead and, with the arrival of the Australians in England, I approached the local pro., a taciturn character from Nottingham. He knew George Gunn personally so here was indeed the oracle. In answer to my anxious inquiry as to how England would fare against the visitors on English pitches, he chewed on his straw for some moments, spat on the grass and turned his cold pale eye upon me. "They'll beat 'em" he said, and proceeded on his way. Although no long and closely reasoned appreciation supported this verdict, it was good enough and one was able to await the day with equanimity.

It came. On the 28th of May, 1921, while Uddingston were locked in combat with a rival Western Union club, there hove into view the huge and portly figure of one C. D. Stuart, a notable Glasgow sports writer. His emblems were a bowler hat and unfurled umbrella, but his whole mien was that of the stricken harbinger from Flodden field. His reactions to a chorus of impatient inquiries were also identical to those of his mediaeval counterpart in that "Thrice he strove to answer, and thrice he groaned aloud". At length in a voice of pain and derision he burst forth "The great England side" he cried— "All out for 112!".

It was not until the rains broke in July of that glorious summer that from Manchester came the glad tidings that for once England, aided by the weather, had the better of a Test Match. This taste of blood, if slightly diluted, was sufficient to send England to the Oval in better heart, where once more a creditable performance raised the morale of the anxious watcher from afar.

The season of 1921 ended with a great treat. Nottingham came to the North and played a series of matches, one of them at Uddingston. The professional for once seemed to be stirred to some slight enthusiasm, and spent weeks preparing a most special wicket, with the express purpose of seeing George Gunn make a hundred on it. There was but one snag. I was a day boy at Glasgow Academy and due to go back before the start of the match so would see little if anything of it; but there is a Guardian Angel who watches over little boys and, every now and then, grants them their dearest wishes by devious means. In this case he used the heavy roller which ran over enough of me, in the shape of my right foot, to prevent me returning to school. I can say with my hand on my heart that this was purely an accident; but psychiatrists would doubtless point out that impending events had made me unduly accident prone.

I saw the whole match and, if George Gunn did not make a hundred, a young man named Whysall made sixty and was pointed out as a coming England batsman, while Fred Barratt seemed to be the world's fastest bowler.

Next year Johnny Douglas brought a representative side to Glasgow and in 1923 Leicester came to Inverness. It must have been about this time that one Harry Rowan, an enthusiastic supporter of cricket, brought Hobbs and Sutcliffe up to his Glasgow store for a week or so. For the price of a pair of batting gloves I was able to talk to both. I remember asking Herbert Sutcliffe to demonstrate his straight drive, of which I'd read, and this he did with great good nature and gusto. For the Master I kept the 64,000 dollar question. I asked how to play the fast leg-break, and was somewhat shocked when he flippantly replied " by walking back to the pavilion ". Be it added that he atoned for this blasphemy by patiently answering a host of similarly testing inquiries.

In 1924 the South Africans came and had an uneasy passage on turf wickets. When they returned home Herbie Taylor was quoted as saying that English cricket was very strong indeed and that Gilligan's team, about to set sail for Australia, should return with the Ashes. This was true hope, and there was always Maurice Tate.

It was rather a raw December evening when I went forth to get the evening paper, and pore over the first day's play in the opening Test Match. It was altogether too precious and exciting a moment to be dissipated by a casual glance in the shop or the street so with superhuman forbearance I carried the paper home unfolded—Test Matches were not then front page news. On arrival I soon found the vital news and gazed at it stunned. Australia were 272 for three.

Collins had made a hundred, as had the newcomer Ponsford. Tate had taken but one wicket despite the fact that, according to the description of play, he had beaten the bat frequently, and troubled every batsman who faced him during the day. The correspondent's views on Tate

were amply borne out the following day, and there was
even better news of the new opening pair Hobbs and Sutcliffe. But the end was again a tale of England's uneven
batting.

Although the issue had been decided there was great
jubilation when England beat Australia in the fourth Test
Match for the first time in 12 years. Alas, this triumphant
course was short-lived for, a few days later, Clarrie Grimmett popped up, like an outsize serpent on a snakes and
ladder board, to put us back where we started.

To a lad who had never seen a first class match these
great events had a powerful and even mystical quality.
One's impressions were derived from reading and studying
photographs and moving pictures. To this was added a
great deal of hearsay, much of it inaccurate, and the whole
brewed up in an imagination made vivid by intense
interest. Having grown familiar with Test Matches and
players over the years the mind sees such matters and persons rather differently but, sometimes, a glance at the old
scores will conjure up within it a delicious and elusive
picture as seen through a boy's eyes. But it is not only the
picture of the busy, aggressive green-capped batsman in-
cessantly harrying the toiling English bowlers on wickets
of grey steel (not an inaccurate image) but the fleeting
nostalgic whiff of longing to be oneself part of an un-
attainable world. Having gained it, if but for a short time,
I wouldn't deny it was everything promised but nothing
could quite equal the magic of the picture as it was originally seen.

Although I had not seen a first class match I had, as I
have said, seen quite a number of first class cricketers in
action. Just as a child, when very young, is inclined to
lump all grown-ups together, I regarded all county
cricketers as a race apart. But, grand as the amateur who
got an occasional game for his county might be, it was
soon apparent that, although he might play against Jack
Hobbs, he wasn't really on the same planet. Still, I felt if
ever I attained such status my life would be complete.

BOWLER'S TURN

And how different was the cricket of the mid-'twenties from that of the 'fifties? I have argued that evolution is much slower than is generally believed and I would say that the cricketer of the 'twenties suddenly set down in the 'fifties would take a comparatively small degree of adjustment. The techniques of playing back or forward, or of spinning or swerving a ball have altered not a jot. There has been no invention such as the googly to nonplus the transplanted batsman and divide his era sharply from the later one. The alteration to the LBW law would, of course, cause him considerable inconvenience in the first instance in itself, and more broadly in its general influence on tactics. The bowler advanced by a time machine would, on the other hand, have been nigh delirious when suddenly acquainted with his increased field of operation.

Both would find the immediate atmosphere much as in their own time, which is to say that, if they played for a cheerful team, there would be the same happy give and take. Circumstances would certainly tend to be very much more democratic, and the relationship between amateur and pro. a trifle surprising to both parties. In the 'twenties the different sects changed in separate dressing rooms in most cases, which had the merit of affording all a bit more elbow room, and occasionally emerged and retired through different gates. The implements would differ in only the smallest details. The ball would be fractionally smaller, and the boots of lighter build. The stumps would be an inch taller and greater in diameter so that, if less elusive, would react in a much less satisfying and spectacular manner when disturbed—when I bowled quick medium even my modest impact once sent one of the old-fashioned stumps cartwheeling twelve or fifteen yards away. When Larwood or Constantine hit the old-fashioned and frailer target the results were really conclusive and worthwhile.

Although the implements and techniques are but little changed over the years their application has developed or degenerated to some extent, according to one's way of thinking. The first element which has brought about a difference in the play is non-technical and one of attitude. With the immense publicity given to Test Matches in particular, and competitive county matches in general, through modern publicity mediums great weight attaches to the result, and great weight is liable to fall on the head of the loser. A Test Match against Australia is no longer a sporting event, it is a " news story ". The unsuccessful side is seldom excused on the grounds of being the less accomplished, but finds itself the subject of all manner of oblique accusations and dark hints. It would seem that no team setting forth from this country can be beaten by a superior side pure and simple. Excess, dissension, prosperity and various corroding influences have robbed it of all vitality. Sometimes it is the fault of blundering officialdom, although in this we may be less severe than the Pakistanis who, at the moment of defeat, gathered in front of the pavilion and cried " Death to the selectors ! "

At any rate the effect of all this is gradual but cumulative—for cricketers are human. A man feels a great weight of responsibility captaining his country, and may already be hardly disposed to take undue risks when he thinks he can achieve his object by safer means which leave an avenue of retreat in case of misfire. With the added threat of universal execration in case of defeat he, and his colleagues, can hardly be blamed if their first determination is not to be beaten.

In the 'twenties sides were just as keen to win. There were never two tougher leaders than Warwick Armstrong and Johnny Douglas. But the point is they wanted to *win* and their outlook was rather " engage the enemy closer " whatever the state of the game. To fall back on wholly defensive tactics was an admission of defeat and generally despised. Therefore the art of completely shutting the game up, if not unknown, was very little practised. The batsman of the 'twenties suddenly transplanted would have found this something of a different world, and a more efficient but a much less attractive one. No-one can blame the bowler, after his rocky and chequered career between these periods, nor altogether the captain in his parlous state, for making full use of the latitude of the law, but I for one think that the resultant curtailment of the leg-side field is infinitely the lesser of two evils, when the other is complete suppression of stroke play.

It should be observed, in passing, that Root bowled a very sharp in-swinger to a most pronounced leg-side field in the 'twenties without unduly restricting the scoring rate. The latter point is endorsed by his figures, and the answer to it is almost certainly the frustrating LBW law as it then stood and possibly the attitude of batsmen of unfettered outlook. And here we debouch upon the field of pure technicality.

Root was so much an exception in the 'twenties that one of the early "colour stories" was to describe him as a "mystery bowler" when he was picked to play for England in 1926. In post-war days the in-swinger became the predominant form of seam attack in England. In the hands of the great artists like Lindwall and Bedser who, by differing means, could also move the ball away from the bat, it was a most potent and aggressive weapon. In the hands of lesser performers it was a negative performance with a numbing effect upon batsmanship. The focus of play became the on-side which could be adequately staffed against such strokes as were possible. This is all very economical and efficient, but these are qualities which can war against attraction, and have done so most effectively as far as cricket is concerned. As I have earlier admitted, I have reluctantly come to the conclusion that, while the alteration to the LBW law has brought a measure of justice to the bowler it has also led him astray. In seeking to exploit its immediate and obvious benefits he has done much to kill off-side stroke play, the greatest joy of cricket, and has influenced the direction of play to the on-side where he can most easily cramp it. In this the slower bowlers have been encouraged by misguided attempts to aid them by deliberately reducing the quality of wickets, which process has been in turn helped by a series of wet summers.

The 'twenties also had their troubles. The standard in England was no doubt rather low upon restarting, as indeed it was after the second world war. The players were not then suspect of moral delinquency but were castigated more on technical grounds, and often quite wrongly. After the destruction wrought by Gregory and McDonald there was a great outcry against the "two-eyed" stance, which, it was said, prevented batsmen playing boldly forward to fast bowling. But the genuine "two-eyed" stance, so-called, was very rare, and it is not possible to play the unvarying forward plunge at fast bowlers who do not consistently over-pitch. As one victim of this advice said with understandable impatience, the most likely result of playing forward at Gregory, with his steep lift off the good length, was to be hit smack in the teeth. The real answer to this, which was equally true twenty-five years later, was that real pace is a major upset to all batsmen who are unaccustomed to it, whether they play back, forward or half-cock. It is always difficult to get safe practise against it and, if there are no fast bowlers in the country, impossible.

The bowlers were roundly denounced for concentrating too much on swerve and thus losing accuracy. They were advised to get back to spin and good length. This was rather a demanding and contradictory order for, while the art of swerving is little removed from that of plain straight bowling and so does nothing to upset control, that of spinning is more complicated and makes length and direction a very much trickier matter. The "googly" was stigmatised in some quarters as a fetish, despite the consistent success of several practitioners. But the real answer was, again, a trough of low pressure following on a period of complete inactivity.

By the mid-'twenties things were pretty good. There was the batting of Hobbs, Woolley and Gunn to lead the younger school of Sutcliffe, Chapman, the Ashtons and, soon to come, Hammond. Tate was in full bloom; the finest fastish seamer of all time, Larwood, wasn't far away. Freeman was the most consistent leg-break and googly

BOWLER'S TURN

bowler in the world, so far as we knew, for Clarrie Grimmett had still to visit this country. Wilfred Rhodes was the finest craftsman amongst the left-handers, and remains so in my memory to this day.

The general aspect was of the ball directed at the off-stump and an off-side field. When bowlers wanted to discourage scoring they bowled wide to the off which still gave the really enterprising striker some scope at increased risk. It was infinitely more elegant than the drab spectacle of a packed leg-side field and the ball pitching outside an impassive batsman's legs.

Perhaps elegance is the outstanding quality in contrast to modern efficiency. The object of all cricketers should now be to assimilate the lessons of all these years, and leaven the increased efficiency with the largely departed elegance.

CHAPTER THREE

Picture of the Year

ONE MORNING I WAS WALKING ALONG A Melbourne street when I ran into a very distinguished citizen, one Richie Benaud. As we passed the time of day he mentioned that he was going to have his hair cut, adding that there hung in the barber's shop a rather interesting old photograph. It was of Sammy Carter catching Jack Hobbs behind the wicket in 1921, a very notable catch. This sounded rather intriguing so I said I would walk along with him and have a look at it.

We were welcomed by the proprietor, Mr. Brown, who had been a member of his profession for a good long time, and had attended to many famous pates, including the variously well thatched ones of Hobbs, Sutcliffe, Hendren and Woolley, the last appropriately named for this particular appointment. He showed us his picture with due pride, for it was indeed a beauty.

Sure enough it was a picture of a very famous moment in the fourth Test which England lost (along with the other four) by eight wickets. The score sheet describes this incident, which occurred in the first innings as " Hobbs c Carter b McDonald 27 ". The caption beneath the photograph describes how Carter, anticipating the stroke, had taken three paces to the off before the ball was struck, and he is shown charging, head down, into the gully. Gregory arrayed, unusually for him, in Australian cap is rolling over in a somersault in the opposite direction, while Armstrong, gigantic and grinning, stands applauding at second slip. Mailey stands at old-fashioned point and favours the sun hat, with Collins at cover, and Kelleway at mid-on. The departing striker wears a felt hat turned down all round, while Makepeace, in cap, presents a dejected back view to the world.

The bowler has also got his back turned, but is readily recognisable by the symmetry of his build and the easy grace of his posture. In the background the crowd, stuffy in blue serge, watch apathetically, for the significance of the scene has not yet burst upon them. Their headgear varies from the black homburg to the panama and this, with the drain-pipe flannels and heavy cricket boots of the players, gives the general aspect of a period piece.

The camera has by chance caught most of the principal actors in the match. Although he only made forty runs all told, Hobbs was always a principal actor. The catcher, re-told, in the fall of six wickets. Armstrong made a hundred, and Gregory seventy-seven and seventy-six not out. Mailey took four for one hundred and fifteen and nine for one hundred and twenty-one, his finest hour. Make-peace made one hundred and seventeen and fifty-four.

But the most fascinating figure of the lot was enjoying one of his few successful moments in the series. Ted McDonald played in three of the five matches, ending with the indifferent record of six wickets for three hundred and ninety-two runs. No matter; the legend runs that every time he missed the bat, which he did with a frequency alto-gether disproportionate to these figures, the watchers grouped around would nod and say "You'll do for Eng-land, son". And he did, in a double sense.

What scenes this old picture could revive in the imagina-tion of the beholder who could span these forty years, and what pangs in his heart. As I have said, there can be no cricketers like those seen through twelve-year-old eyes, and for me the Australian side of 1921 is still the greatest of all cricket teams. It may well be the greatest in fact, if not the most formidable. It was certainly one of the most attractive. The batting was lively and of the highest quality, led by Charlie Macartney, the "Governor General" himself. When Bardsley and Collins had got the shine off there was also Andrews, Taylor, Armstrong and Gregory, all players of strokes, the last two of particularly forceful strokes. The bowling was confined to four top-class bowlers, all of whom appear in our picture. Of all fast bowling combinations my favourite is Gregory and McDonald. Whether it was the best in terms of absolute efficiency I wouldn't know, but it could not have been far off, when the breeze blew from the proper quarter. It was certainly the most picturesque in my span, and the partners were so perfectly contrasted as to be exactly complementary. The same could be said of the slow bowlers, for Armstrong's consistent accuracy and economical turn was as far removed from Mailey's vast spin and variable pitch as two performances could be and still belong to the same category.

For this particular beholder to conjure up the most beautiful feature of the scene, Hobbs v. McDonald, it is necessary to alloy a vivid but separate memory of each with pure imagination for, although I saw and played with the most perfect of fast bowlers and the most polished of batsmen, I never actually saw them in opposition; at least in their hey-day. In fact the occasions upon which they met at top level were confined to the few of the 1920-21 series, six in all, for in 1921 Hobbs, dogged by injury and ill-health, took no actual part in any match. When the next series was played McDonald was a Lancastrian. They met a great many times as county cricketers, but that has hardly got the same dramatic quality.

I do, or did, know all of those present with two exceptions, Carter and Kelleway who, like several others present, finished their mortal innings some time ago. But the memories of those who have departed remain delightfully fresh here and in their native land. Talking of what was to me a great discovery in the club that evening, I was rewarded by much reminiscence of Warwick Armstrong supplied by a younger, but contemporary, cricketer. Not of the tough, awe-inspiring conqueror, but of the Falstaff with a love of life, and a generous twinkle in his eye at such moments as, when struck for three fours by the narrator, he warned him to be "very careful", before dispatching him with a top spinner, slyly disguised. There was a glorious glimpse of Carter, an undertaker, in the transitional stage between business and pleasure, arriving in the nick of time for a club match, and swopping top hat for cricket cap on the box of a four-in-hand hearse at full gallop.

Happily there is a goodly remnant of this incomparable army. Jack Gregory, a magnificent and upright figure, is a trustee of the Sydney Cricket Ground, and was there to welcome May's team and the press at a recent gathering. Between 1919 and 1922 he rivalled his captain as the greatest all-rounder in the world and, on his form of that period, must rank pretty high amongst the all-rounders of all time. But it was not so much what he did but the immense agile gusto with which he did it that made him the biggest drawing card of his era. If I was given the chance of seeing once again any single cricketer bat, bowl and field I would choose to see Gregory well ahead of any other performer within my ken.

Arthur Mailey, whimsical, witty and provocative, adorns the press box when the mood takes him and not when it doesn't. The last time I was in Sydney Herbie Collins sat amongst friends, dapper with bow tie and Tyrolean hat, but died some months ago. And if they do not appear in the picture Nip Pellew and Johnny Taylor were somewhere in the deep. Nip is coach to South Australia, brown haired, broad and strong, and said to have an appetite which is the envy of his lustiest charges.

Johnny Taylor I last saw in London where, having got him to lunch, by dint of a glass or two of wine and much prodding and urging I prevailed upon him to talk a bit about himself and the great days. It was amply worth while. Jack Ryder is a selector of mature years, but he remembers with especial pleasure the hundred he made in Glasgow on Warwick Armstrong's tour. It must have been a pretty good one because I can see most of it now forty years on.

PICTURE OF THE YEAR

Of the strikers Jack Hobbs is as good a 77 as they come. He lives down on the South Coast but still attends his London business several days a week and a great many cricket functions as well. His partner, Harry Makepeace, died some years ago when coach to his native county, after a long and honourable career for county and country. To now grizzled Lancastrians, Makepeace and Hallows are names as hallowed and inseparable as Rolls and Royce.

The hairdressers in Mr. Brown's shop are also men of mature years. Ever and anon as they shear the heads of the young lions they must raise their eyes to the wall and sigh. Mr. Brown says that his picture, for reasons of age, cannot be reproduced. For ought I know there is something symbolical in this.

CHAPTER FOUR

The Enthusiast

IN DAYS GONE BY LIONEL TENNYSON, following in the wake if not exactly the footsteps of his illustrious grandparent, was wont to recite an ode of his own composition on the subject of love. I cannot quote it verbatim; but it posed the question as to which was the most sublime of all forms of love—the love of a mother for her child, the burning youth for his maid, or the patriot for his country. The conclusion reached in the last two profoundly moving lines was that the greatest of all was " the infinite, tender, compassionate love of one dead drunk for another ".

Whether one agreed with this verdict or not, the poem contained one serious omission. It failed to mention one very strong runner for a place in the scale of devotion, and that was the love of a man for his chosen game. The chap who sleeps on the pavement the night before a Test Match; or he who bawls himself into premature apoplexy with cries of "Feet, Scotland, Feet", have a pure devotion only partially sustained by alcohol. Even the gentleman who calls for the immediate and violent end of the ref. (apparently on account of the official's morals and parentage as well as his defective judgement) has love as well as hate in his heart.

My own experience is chiefly confined to the cricket variety of fanatic; but of these I have known many. In fact so many that it would be unfair, and indeed impossible, to award pride of place to any individual. But for a single act of devotion the highest decoration must go to one who was a familiar figure at Lord's in pre-war days. His name I never knew but he was always readily identifiable by his heavy moustache, pince-nez and a black boater which he sported in all weathers.

On this particular occasion he was sitting nearby when a rather dull county match came to an end, just after lunch on the third day. Fishing out a heavy gold Albert he sat for a few moments in deep thought then, turning to his neighbour, said "If I catch the next train I might just see the last hour at Trent Bridge," with which he upped and off.

My curiosity and admiration aroused, I later looked in the evening paper and saw that Trent Bridge had been an even duller match, with Charlie Harris defending stolidly for the last hour, in order to ensure a draw. Doubtless the traveller derived much pleasure from this, and one could imagine him ruminating happily on the return journey, and enjoying an occasional glimpse of an evening match as he sped homewards to a cosy half hour with Wisden before retiring for the night.

It was about this time that an honoured and august spectator returned, if but fleetingly, to Lord's. In his late sixties Aubrey Smith, his fame as a cricketer and an actor forgotten, had gone to Hollywood unnoticed and without any very lively hope. A few years later he returned to his native land to make a film, world famous, wealthy and a knight. Such was the respect he commanded in his profession that, rumour had it, he stipulated in his contract that he would be released from duty every time the Australians played at Lord's. At any rate he was always there.

His renown meant little to his fellow members. An elderly member, listening a trifle impatiently to his resonant comments on the play, turned to his companion. "Who's this fella with the loud voice?" he enquired.

"Hmmm" replied his fellow member, after a prolonged scrutiny. "Fella named Smith—used to play for Sussex".

Another most illustrious lover of the game of cricket is Mr. R. G. Menzies. Although he can hardly take leave from his immense duties he does manage his affairs so adroitly that his visits to this country frequently coincide with a Test Match series. Even so pressure of events can

thwart him at any time. It was a most enlightening gesture,
therefore, on the part of officialdom to have a television
set installed in his official car in order that he might watch
the play as he journeyed on the business of state while in
this country.

As cricket devotees are happily drawn from every creed
and strata there are those who cannot mould circumstance
to the fixture list. The most exciting match I ever played
in was against Bermuda and such was the enthusiasm that
we drew a third of the population on the day of the match.
Perhaps the two most deserving spectators had spent between them nigh forty years in the employment of a fruit
store. The day before the contest the boss, in somewhat
sadistic jest, said he was going to the match so they would
have to mind the shop. There was dreadful consternation
at this and his faithful adherents, having put their woolly
heads together, returned to announce with dignity and regret that they jointly resigned forthwith. This the boss
countered by saying that, on the contrary, they were
sacked—until the day after the match.

The trouble with the active participant is, on the other
hand, to prevail upon him to resign in any circumstances;
for it is when scarcely active any more that he realises how
precious his associations are and the full agony that
parting will be. The status of the individual matters not a
jot, for most of the professionals I have known have played
primarily for the love of the game, and have been deeply
grateful that it has incidentally provided a means of livelihood. Cricket does not bring great riches to any but the
stars, but few of the less successful would be suborned by
the prospect of more lucrative if infinitely less rewarding
employment. Many have even refused advancement offered
by other counties because of roots grown deep in familiar
surroundings and companionship.

The most painful deprivation in my experience, however, befell an amateur, and probably the most industrious
cricketer in the history of the game. Being of independent
means he was able to indulge his passion for the game

without restraint. Throughout the season he never played less than two matches a day and, on really propitious days, was able to work in a third late in the evening. It was a singularly unpropitious day when, in running a quick single, he had sustained a badly strained leg muscle. The cream of Harley Street were called, confessed that they were unable to accelerate the processes of nature, and the injured man retired to his club in a deep gloom. In answer to a sympathetic friend's enquiry he estimated his recovery would take about three weeks.

"That's a long time" said the friend. "I'll bet you will miss quite a few matches".

"I shall," replied the invalid. "In fact I've had to cancel fifty-six already".

As I write I am packing my bags for a first visit to the West Indies and a request for guidance and information addressed to my old fellow-traveller Bob Wyatt brought to light an enthusiast who, in a rather more flamboyant vein, rivalled my friend who went to Trent Bridge. Bob took the M.C.C. side to the West Indies in 1934 and was first aware of his admirer when the ship, approaching Barbados, dropped anchor a mile off-shore. A figure, ebony and dripping, having swum the distance unaided, and shinned up the cable, arrived beaming in the midst of the official welcome to assure Captain Wyatt that no introductions were necessary for he knew all present. Aided this time by a helpful send off from the bo'sun, he made the return journey by the same route, but was early in evidence the following day. Meeting the team's cars some distance from the ground he ran before them, a self-appointed unmounted out-rider, waving the Union Jack and cheering his head off until, through nervous and physical exhaustion, he fell smack on his face. This performance he repeated daily, scornful of thrombosis or appearances, and always winding up prone by the wayside. However, as soon as his legs would support him, he would make his way to the ground and, when Captain Wyatt made a hundred, was on hand to see that this feat did not pass unrecognised. A hastily organised and unofficial committee rushed on to the field to bear the centurion shoulder high. What matter that, owing to excitement and official interference, the only parts of the hero's anatomy accessible to those eager hands were his ankles, so that he was borne triumphantly all right— but upside down with his head bumping painfully on the ground, and occasionally trodden on by a friendly bare foot.

But then Bob is a great enthusiast and, once recovered from the ceremony, was the first to appreciate the spirit behind it. I hope the instigator survives with a vast tribe of progeny who have his enthusiasm—not to say lack of inhibition.

CHAPTER FIVE

Battle *Royal*

STRICTLY SPEAKING MY NEXT BRIEF IS to write about the great players and occasions since the 1930s, but as both, in many cases, had their roots and origins in earlier times it may be convenient to start with the M.C.C. tour of South Africa in 1927-28, which was my first continuous incursion into first-class cricket. I should perhaps explain how I came to go there at all, being previously unheard of. It is a tale which almost belongs to the realm of "Fifty Best Stories for Boys".

When I was secretary to Aubrey Faulkner at his cricket school I used to bowl the leg-break on his indoor pitches at a round fast-medium pace, and turn it quite a way. Although I say so, it really was quite an exceptional ball, and I reckoned that only very good players who had seen something of me could keep me out on this particular wicket. It was a performance which filled Faulkner with pride and joy, even if my efforts as a secretary drove him almost to despair.

I had another most loyal supporter in Sir Pelham Warner and both most generously sang my praises in high quarters. As a result, it was decided to take me with the M.C.C. party in the guise of secretary to the captain, as he then was, Captain R. T. Stanyforth. Knowing my powers of disorganisation in matters of office routine, Faulkner must have had a twinge of conscience over this, but everyone, including the captain, seemed to regard it as a most satisfactory arrangement. It can readily be imagined that I was nigh stunned by the excitement of it all.

The series was really the end of an era, in that it was the last in which all matches were played upon matting wickets. No doubt it was inevitable that the South Africans should change to turf, and so be on equal terms with

39

the other major cricket powers, but it was not without some loss. Allowing for the fact that I was very young and my judgement immature, I still remember the cricket on the fast matting wicket at Johannesburg as the greatest and most exciting duel between batsman and bowler in all the play I have seen in 30 years.

Many complain that the unchanging conditions of a matting wicket make for monotony, but to my mind this is not entirely true and, even if so, is easily outweighed in this case by the fact that the pitch gave both batsman and bowler full scope for their respective skills. The ball would always turn quickly but consistently, and the surface was absolutely fair and predictable to the batsman.

The South Africans at this time had a splendid side, bred on matting wickets. The bowling was led by George Bissett who, in short bursts, was one of the really fast bowlers of all time. Denys Morkel would help to get the shine off, and this he did most gracefully with a high, flowing action, after which the stage would be set for the arrival of "Buster" Nupen.

Nupen was purely a matting-wicket bowler and, on the mat, something of a phenomenon. In his prime he was a beautifully built man of around six feet, very blond and, owing to an accident when young, one-eyed. He ran about eight yards and bowled with a rhythmical slinging arm, which followed a pattern not unlike that of Tyson.

In pace he would be perhaps a shade slower than Bedser. His stock ball was a tremendous off-break which fairly whipped back off the mat, so much so that one batsman complained that, every time he tried to off-drive him, he was liable to lose the seat of his pants. By way of variation he bowled a cutter which went a few inches the other way, and that also flew from the pitch. And here is one of the inherent virtues of the mat. The unskilled batsman found it almost impossible to pick the break from the bowler's hand and so was, quite rightly, confounded. The skilled could detect the break and anticipate it, but even so found it fully testing.

In support came two left-handers, Cyril Vincent, a beautiful spinner of the ball at medium pace, and Alfie Hall, rather quicker, with a low action which ensured his hitting the castle whereas, with the higher arm, the ball was liable to bounce over.

To combat this array we had four top-class professional batsmen, Holmes, Sutcliffe, Tyldesley and Hammond. There was then a youthful Wyatt still in the development stage, but after that would come the avalanche. When the experts were at grips it was a real battle royal. The rate of scoring hardly seemed to matter; for, with this superb attack well directed and pressed right home by "Nummy" Deane, every ball had the quality of life and death.

Percy Holmes was the most cheerful and ebullient of all opening batsmen. When he left the ball alone there was more animation in this negative exercise than in many batsmen hitting a four. He leapt high into their air, touching down with both feet outside the off stump, the bat flailing high overhead, in the manner of a cannon-ball service, to end in a crouching posture, grinning broadly, maybe at the bowler's wasted effort, maybe just for the joy of batting. His spirits never flagged.

In the last Test Match at Durban he made nought in the first innings (caught Cameron, bowled Bissett) and I see him now, sitting with his pads on waiting to open our second go, dapper, smiling, happy. There was, naturally, a good deal of backchat and some malicious suggestions that Bissett was just too good and quick for a batsman of mature years. It was not to be expected that these sallies would have any effect whatsoever and, as he took his leave, our hope for runs to come turned beaming to the company. "I could play this Bissett with a bludy broom 'andle", he said and was gone.

A resounding smack, followed by a louder appeal, decided the issue in the first over. Holmes (l.b.w., bowled Bissett o) bounced back in an unaffected aura of bonhomie, to announce, with every appearance of satisfaction, that it was the first time he had bagged 'em. Thereafter Ewart

BOWLER'S TURN

Astill, a notable player of the ukelele, altered the words of his theme song to read:

"If a duck is your luck never mind
Poor old Percy will get two, you will find".

At the other end Herbert Sutcliffe took a little time to get wholly used to the behaviour of the mat but was ever calm and determined. When one or other of the Yorkshire pair was despatched his place was taken by Ernest Tyldesley, who usually batted number three, ahead of Wally Hammond. Like his brother "J.T.", before him, Tyldesley was one of the best-liked and most respected cricketers of his generation. He is a seriously-minded man, though with a nice humour, and made a perfect head professional. With Ronnie Stanyforth as captain we were at least splendidly led and a very happy and orderly party.

Ernest was probably at his very best on the matting. The reduction, or perhaps more correctly, advancement of the game to an exact science suited his particular technique to perfection. He had two peculiarities for a great player. He picked the bat up and, more importantly, brought it down from a point in the direction of third man and when he hooked he was not always outside the line of the ball.

It was said these flaws occasionally betrayed him on turf wickets, although his record would hardly suggest that they did. At any rate, on matting, with its consistent pace and bounce, they certainly did not, and his hook was a powerful stroke which used to send the ball scudding away rather between square-leg and long-on. He fought some wonderful duels with each of the bowlers I have named, and averaged 65 in the Test Matches.

Walter Hammond had just recovered from a very severe illness, contracted while on tour in the West Indies, and was in the process of re-establishing himself in the very front rank of international batsmen. He not only batted with great success, foreshadowing his stupendous Australian success a year ahead, but was a very hostile bowler. With Constantine, he was the greatest all-round fielder in the game and at Capetown he ran the great Herbie Taylor out by fielding the ball somewhere in the region of mid-on off his own bowling and throwing the wicket down, all in one enormous cat-like burst of agility.

The only other batsman who met with much success was Bob Wyatt, then twenty-six and a magnificent batsman, if not quite fully matured. He must rank in the first half-dozen English amateurs since the end of the first world war and was my half-section, guide, mentor and instructor on all matters on and off the field. He had, and continues to have, strong and thoughtful views on an astonishing variety of subjects and a wonderful sense of humour, which at first took some digging out from behind an impassive countenance.

When four of our champions had been despatched an end was always open and, as Wally Hammond said, you could hear the bowlers' ears go back with a click. The slaughter was at least swift and painless; for in that fierce temperature there was no respite for mug or martyr. Patience, such a virtue on the doped turf wicket, was not enough, and the dull and drab were snuffed out as quickly as they came. The measure of our destruction can be gauged by the fact that the next name on the batting averages after the big five was that of Peebles.

Easily our best bowler was George Geary, another of the great characters who abound in the cricket world. In pace he was a sharp quick medium, a most dangerous bowler on damaged wickets and a thoroughly reliable and dependable performer on plumb ones. He had a large capacious hand which admirably concealed his intentions, which were, as in the case of Nupen, an off-break varied by a leg-cutter.

The first was not so ferocious as that of his South African rival, but the leg one was both better-controlled and better-concealed, a very deadly ball indeed as soon as the pitch would bite. Geary's pace and methods were ideally suited to the matting, and he completely destroyed a strong South African batting side in the first Test Match at Johannesburg, taking twelve wickets for 130 and winning the match for his side. An injury to his elbow kept him out for much of the tour, and we never recovered from this loss.

At this time Herbie Taylor was still going strong, regarded by many as the world's best batsman on his own home grounds. He was a model for any young player. The pick-up of the bat was mathematically straight, his judgement of length perfect, and he had a cardinal attribute in that when he played forward he was at full stretch and, when he played back, he made so much ground that his heels almost touched the stumps.

When very young he had been the only South African batsman to resist the otherwise irresistible Sydney Barnes on matting wickets. He was a very good, indeed great, player on turf, but never quite achieved the same ascendency as he established in his own country.

Despite their poorish showing on the turf wickets of England three years earlier the South Africans were a very good all round side on their own pitches. In addition to Herbie Taylor they had a number of top class batsmen on the mat. Bob Catterall was a fine opening batsman with lots of strokes which he played with the full open face of the bat. In the outfield he rivalled "Nip" Pellew in that he was an even timer with a beautiful economical action, and a sure quick-fire return. Amongst other talents he was also a most accomplished performer on the ukelele, a very fashionable instrument at that time. A left-hander named Nicholson was a player in the Phil Mead mould and a thorn in our sides, and it was strange that his career seemed to consist almost solely of this one series. Denys Morkel was a fine upstanding driver of the ball, and "Nummy" Deane showed the same fine cheerful determination at the crease as he did in all circumstances whilst leading his side. Ten South African batsmen averaged over twenty as against five serious performers on our side. The

My own part in the proceedings was a modest one. The co-ordination essential to the quick leg-break I had perfected indoors still eluded me, and I settled for the fastish

44

off-break and occasional leg-break and googly. With these I was fairly successful in the matches against the Provinces, but not very effective in the Tests.

My enjoyment of the trip was enormous and unbelieving, as well it might have been. At 19 I was extremely gangling, gauche and shy; very young indeed for my age. Both sides regarded me with a sort of paternal amusement, pulled my leg like mad, and were wonderfully kind. When I naïvely sought instruction on how to bowl the leg-cutter from the famous and respected "Buster" Nupen he gave it freely, as though to a younger brother. In a Test Match I made 26 in time of crisis and two and a half hours, which must have been an unendurable trial to the opposition, and I still remember, in the intensity of the battle, "Nummy" Deane good-naturedly addressing me as "Stonewall Jackson" and saying I was a ruddy nuisance.

Indeed the spirit of this series was wonderfully good throughout, for the respective captains both gave their sides a splendid lead and example in how to do your darndest without rancour. It was certainly an object lesson to those who, in cricket, believe in the puerile attitude of hating the enemy on and off the field.

I finished the cricket part of the trip with a notable if unintended feat. Reporting a delightful up country match the *Cape Times* described my contribution as "absent bathing o." I returned to this country having learned quite a bit about cricket and, maybe, a modicum about life.

CHAPTER SIX

The Cloth

A FEW DAYS BEFORE HE TOOK HOLY Orders, around a couple of hundred years ago, Henry Venn gave his bat away. He did so in the interests of decorum, for, said he, never would he gladly hear the cry " Well hit, Parson ". This may seem a strange gesture and explanation to modern eyes and ears for it is surely a warming and friendly cry, and a most frequent one since The Rev. Henry's misgiving.

The next clergyman to figure prominently in cricket history was of rather different character and a good deal less fussy. A boyhood portrait of The Rev. Lord Frederick Beauclerk shows a face which in its innocent beauty would have been conspicuous amongst the angels. It is a regrettable fact that his behaviour on an angelic cricket field might well have been equally so. Although he did much to further the game, his approach seems to have been hot tempered and mercenary but successful, for he reckoned cricket was annually worth six hundred guineas to him in stakes and side bets. His peremptory " Play or pay Sir " to an ailing Squire Osbaldeston smacks more of the Kremlin than the M.C.C., let alone Convocation House. There is a most unholy satisfaction to be derived from the reflection that he lost his match and money when Lambert, as crafty as he, bowled a series of wides " to put him out of temper ".

It is pleasant to record that from then on all the clergy seem to have played the game with the decorum which Venn applauded, and some with considerable distinction. The Rev. W. Fellows figures gloriously, if briefly, in Wisden, having while at practice on the Christ Church ground at Oxford, struck the ball 175 yards, from hit to pitch. So

46

swift and sure was The Rev. Vernon Royle at cover that Tom Emmett refused to run when the ball was struck in that direction, remarking to his partner that the "Policeman" was at his post. There was also the parson who achieved anonymous and rather negative fame in having his "pulpit" somewhat blasphemously removed by Crossland's third ball after two near misses and (as the result of a severe warning regarding the customers' susceptibilities) two compressed and sulphurous silences.

But quite apart from being in poor taste the unguarded expression in such company can be, to say the least of it, unprofitable. The Rev. J. H. Parsons of Warwickshire decreed that anyone who spoke opprobrious words upon the field of play should be summarily fined sixpence per word, the proceeds to go to his boys' club. As the financier, in addition to being a powerful straight driver, was blessed with extremely sharp hearing, the system proved most lucrative. So much so, that our captain, a shrewd judge of such markets, was eventually content to settle for one pound, cash on the barrel head, before we started.

The church was fairly generously represented amongst the counties in pre-war days. Middlesex boasted Killick and Hants had Steele and Bridger. Although he was no longer active the name of Gillingham was revered throughout Essex. Payton followed his father to Nottingham, having graduated from Cambridge. The retiring Dean of Westminster, Dr. Don, once made a hundred for Fifeshire.

There were, and are, of course, many purely clerical occasions. In pre-war days the clergy of London grappled annually at Lord's with their brethren of Southwark. One of these fixtures drew but one spectator who sat in solitary state before the tavern. The weather was a trifle inclement and, even though admission was free, the fielding side felt that this fidelity should not go unnoticed. Accordingly, at the fall of the next wicket a deputation advanced down the hill to offer a few words of welcome and gratitude. The "gate" received the deputation with every courtesy but said that he was bound in honesty to say, especially in view

BOWLER'S TURN

of the players' calling, that he had not been unaware that a match was in progress. But, he added, that he found it a pleasant accompaniment to the original purpose of his visit, which was, in fact, the all day licence. It was at a later date that one of the contesting sides discovered that all present had attained their half century in years if not in runs. One of their number suggested it might provide additional inspiration if, on taking the field, they were to intone "O God our help in ages past ".

There is only one case, so far as I know, of a clerical cricketer developing doubts about the game. The story has no less authority than Lord Cobham whose ancestor, The Rev. and Hon. Edward Lyttelton, conceived an inexplicable antipathy towards cricket in his later years when he had become Headmaster of Eton (not that these matters were in any way connected). This was a matter of grief and bewilderment of his family who frequently sought to reason with him to no avail. He made but one trifling concession. Pressed to recant in one instance he relented for a passing moment. "I will confess," he said, "that I never enter the nave of a cathedral without visualising the spin of the ball up the aisle ". As one who liked brick hard or matting wickets, I can see his point.

Although religious prejudice and intolerance may not be unknown in certain sporting spheres it is happily absent in English cricket. The only instance of denominational pride in my experience was far from sinful. It occurred when Middlesex played Hampshire and The Rev. Tom Killick, maybe the best batsman of a pretty good lot, made fifty. Many of these he struck from the bowling of The Rev. J. W. J. Steele, but honours were even when he had his middle stump knocked down. On his return I enquired what sort of stuff his rival bowled. The defeated striker smiled the smile of a happy and contented man. "Good old Church of England " he said—" straight up and down and no nonsense".

And lastly, on the same theme, a tale with a moral.

48

While England lament the absence of Sheppard, Scotland rejoice in the presence of Aitchison, a minister of the "Auld Kirk," a fact not only appropriate but important to this story. Mr. Aitchison has taken a packet of runs off all comers, and when Worcestershire went North he smote their bowlers not only hip and thigh, but with what appeared to the victims to be an altogether undue share of good fortune. His eventual downfall may have been less fortunate for he was rash enough to mention as he retired that he thought he had been unlucky. At this an exasperated Jenkins blew his top. "Unlucky?", he said, "If I had your luck I wouldn't be plain Reverend—I'd be the blooming Archbishop of Canterbury"!

Which only goes to show how disastrous can be the intrusion of lay opinions into ecclesiastical matters, a sentiment which, of course, goes for cricket writers too.

CHAPTER SEVEN

Happy Ending

ASSISTANT DRESSING ROOM ATTENDANT at Loamton ground, said Mr. Dumble, were a chap named Albert Hobley. He were a little chap with a bald 'ead and a very solemn face and though he were a very good worker he were that simple that you might say he were a natural.

Cricket were t'passion of 'is life and when we practised at nets he would coom out and field all day. Theer was noothin' he wouldn't try and stop though, as he seldom got his 'and to ball, he were usually bruised very bad by t'end of it. As a reward we used to give 'im 10 minutes battin' and whole staff would coom to wotch, cos he were that bad and that serious that it were comic to see. Everywoon would fair bust tryin' not to laff so he always thought he was doing fine and, though his bones moost 'ave ached terrible, his feelings were never 'urt. And he would go back to his old moother, wot he lived with, and tell her how noon of t'county could get 'im out.

He was liked very mooch but, being that simple, yoong chaps were always havin' a game with 'im and telling 'im to keep practising and he'd play for England. But he'd say very solemn that maybe at 40 he's a bit old for Test Matches, but he'd fine like a game for t'County. Meantime he has to stroogle to keep his place int village side.

They pulls his leg on all manner o' things, but when they tell 'im that Mrs. Trolley, t'widow lady wot roons bar, has got her eye on 'im he gets very angry, and says that such talk is not respectable-like. But meself I'm not sure theers not soom truth int.

Well time cooms when Albert's old mother oops and dies and t'poor chap's very sad and lost bein' left all by himself. And Mr. Borrington, our skipper, wots a man with a real kind 'eart and very well meanin', is mooch concerned and he cooms to me.

" Dick " he says " I'm mooch concerned about Albert cos this has been a great blow to him, and I'm afraid hes took it very bad. Hes been a reet good and faithful servant to us, and I think we should do summat for him in his adversity ".

And I says " Aye, hes a very deservin' chap. Wot would you suggest? ".

" Well " he says " I were thinkin' we might play match against his village. We could see he made soom roons, and had a nice collection. It would cheer him oop, and maybe he would settle down and marry Mrs. Trolley ".

I haven't mooch faith in Skipper as match maker, except int cricketin' sense, but it seems a good idea ootherwise, so we sets to and arranges fixture.

Match proves great success and whole village turns out when we bat first and give 'em soom nice hittin'. We've arranged with local captain to put Albert on when 7 wickets are down, so he can do hat trick with last three. Our tail-enders never make a roon in their lives, but when they 'ears they're to make a Roman 'oliday for Albert they get very steamed oop, and say they'll never hear end ont. But Skipper bullies and bribes 'em, and sure enoof Albert does 'at trick. Its foony kind of 'at trick cos last chap has to knock his own stoomps down, as ball happens to be a wide.

When they bats Albert cooms in noomber 7 and makes 25 not out. Hes bowled out woonce or twice, but t'oom-pire says " No ball " and when hes roon out accidental t'oother un says he thought it were boundary, and has already signalled four. But Albert is that 'appy he sees nowt o' this and when he cooms off field village band plays " Hail t' conquerin' 'ero cooms! " He gets nice collection, wot he turns over to Quillbeck, t'lawyer, to look after for 'im; but he keeps enoof to stand entire coompany an alf pint after match.

BOWLER'S TURN

Everywoon congratulates him, and chap named Alfie Hustleton wot thinks hes very foony, cooms and slaps 'im ont back.

"Well played, Albert" he says "You're a made man. They'll have to ask you to play for county after that".

And Albert smiles very modest and says he had a bit of luck but he's reet pleased joust t'same. Skipper cooms oop at that moment and he says.

"Good bye now Albert" he says "You've had a great day and, as we're away for next two matches, you'd better have a week's 'oliday to put your affairs in order".

Albert says thanks very mooch, and off we goes to Bailton for t'next match.

Next home match I'm coomin int pavilion when Skipper calls for me. He's got letter in his 'and and hes very poozled.

"'Ere Dick" he says "Wots to do? Soomwoons havin' a joke with us." and he hands me letter wot says.

Dear Sir,

I have to thank you for your kind letter inviting me to play against Blockshire. I have mooch pleasure in accepting and will be theer at 11 o'clock on June 21st as requested.

Yours respectfully,
Albert Hobley.

"Its Albert's writin'" I says "Where was it sent to?"

"It was waiting for me when I got 'ere" he says.

"Well" I says "Its not sort o' joke woon of our chaps 'ud play on Albert, but I have a notion who might ha' doon it".

"So have I" says Skipper "Wot are we goin' to do if he turns oop? It'll break his 'eart if he finds its a joke".

At that moment theers great bustle int passage and in cooms Albert in his best suit. Behind 'im cooms commissionaire smilin' and winkin' and carrying brand new bag as big as Albert himself. We says "Good Mornin'" as genial as we can and Albert says "Good mornin'".

"Joust put my bag down int corner, my man" he says to commissionaire, and when we sees its got printed on it "A. Walton Hobley, Loamshire XI" we don't know whether to laff or cry.

"That's a fine bag" says Skipper "have you joost bought it?".

"Yes sir" says Albert "Mr. Hustleton arranged with sports shop to give me completely new outfit. Did you get my letter all reet?" he says.

"Letter?" says Skipper "Oh aye, o'course, yes. Now" he says very bloof "Make yourself at home for a minute Albert. Dick and me have woon or two things to arrange".

So we go int passage and we dont reetly know wot to do, but as we're talking along cooms Dr. Broom. Skipper explains to 'im wots happened and Dr. Broom says whoever doon it its a miserable kind of joke.

"Could you disqualify 'im on medical grounds?" says Skipper, all of a sooden, "It would anyway spare his feelin's".

Dr. Broom looks a bit doubtful at first but we argues with 'im and says that Albert's sooch a sickly wee chap anyway that hes bound to find summat t'matter with 'im. Doctor says very well then he'll do his best.

We goes back int dressing room and Skipper says very casual "Have you got your invitation on you Albert?" and Albert fishes it out very proud, and we sees its on County note paper with very scribbly signature with oonderneath "For Captain Loamshire XI".

"I see clerks forgot to mention medical examination" says Skipper 'Never mind though, Dr. Broom will roon over you now. We have to do this with all our players, you know".

So Dr. Broom cooms in with his little bag he keeps handy ont ground, and he goes over Albert very thorough. When hes doon he looks very serious like.

"Albert" he says "I'm afeard I've got soom reet bad news for you. You're a very sick man".

"D'ye mean I can't play, sir?" says Albert very took aback.

BOWLER'S TURN

"Not on any account" says Doctor "And wots more you're going to rest oop for a time. Is theer anywoon at 'ome to look after you?".

"No" says Albert, very sad.

"Hum" says Doctor "We'll see wot we can do for you. Get your clothes on now and take it easy".

"Bad Luck" says Skipper "But we moost get you fit for your first match. Anyway" he says "You'll sit with players int mornin' and have loonch with us".

And Albert brightens oop a bit at that, and puts 'is jacket on and goes and sits ont players' balcony.

"Thanks Doctor" says Skipper "You got us out of a very awkward hole. But werent you a bit severe?".

"Jim" says Dr. Broom "All wot I said was true, and its likely a deal worse than that. I'm going to get him int General 'ospital but I doubt they can do owt but make 'im comfortable".

"Wot d'ye mean?" says Skipper "Is he a goner?".

"Very likely" says Doctor "Now get on with your business and let me get to mine".

We're completely stooned to 'ear this, but we do as Doctor says and match starts as though noothin' had 'appened. Albert sits with players and signs autograph books, and soomtimes members coomin' int pavilion waves to 'im, and he nods back very solemn and important. When loonch cooms Skipper tells 'im to sit nearby and asks his advice about pitch and bowlin' and all. Its greatest day in Albert's life, and when Dr. Broom tells 'im its time to coom with him he says "Good Bye All".

"I'll be quite glad o' t'rest" he says "Cos I've felt pretty bad soomtimes last few weeks, but I thought when I were asked to play for t'County I would throw it off".

Well at end of day Skipper and I goes to bar behind free stand where we know we can find Alfie Hustleton. He's theer with soom of his cronies so Skipper oops to him and says "You'll be glad to know our new player turned oop all reet".

And Alfie laffs very 'earty.

"I took a lot o' troable to get 'im for you" he says "Was he satisfactory?".

"Theers nowt satisfactory about it" says Skipper, soodenly very 'ot "And I don't think its goin' to be very satisfactory for you neither".

"Can't you take a joke" says Alfie, a bit took aback.

"That I can" says Skipper "And I hope you can too, cos I think you've got woon cooming to you".

"Wot are you going to do about it?" says Alfie, nasty.

"I don't know" says Skipper "Not till I've showed your letter to Mr. Quillbeck, t'lawyer. Coom on Dick".

Well at end of match couple of days later Skipper and me goes round to t'General 'ospital to see Albert. Dr. Broom has got 'im a wee room to 'imself, and afore we go in Sister says hes soonk very rapid, and we moosnt stay too long. Then she opens t'door and says

"Here are two of your team mates, Mr. Hobley" and as she goes out she says to Skipper so as Albert can 'ear "Its not often we have responsibilty o' nursing a Loamshire cricketer".

He's pretty far gone but at that his eyes light oop and he smiles at us. And Skipper tells 'im to hurry oop and get well but he doesn't seem to grasp mooch and goes babblin' on in a faint kind of a voice. So far as we can 'ear its all about 'ow when he was a wee boy his moother said he was going to be a county cricketer, and wot a pity she had joust missed seein' it 'appen. Then he grows fainter and presently we sees hes fallen asleep lookin' very 'appy, and its time for us to go. Its last time we sees 'im and after a week we hears hes gone.

Well that werent quite t'end of joke, cos Albert leaves a will sayin' all his effects and cash from collection he leaves to Mrs. Trolley, as he was goin' to propose to 'er when match were over. And Quillbeck, who surprises everywoon by dealing with matter free o' charge, gets bill from sports shop chap for £18 7s. 8d. but he answers 'im with soom tremendous Latin words, wot means rooffy he can get 'is mooney out of Alfe Hustleton or whistle for

BOWLER'S TURN

it. And everything turns out quite well as Alfie pays oop
when Quillbeck says, very sinister, that its a lot less than
leastest penalty for forgery.

But I think meself that Skipper were near t'truth when
he says it were a small price to pay for making a man's
last days his 'appiest.

On a Length

CHAPTER EIGHT

The Thirties

NINETEEN-TWENTY-NINE WAS MY FIRST
season of county cricket and I remember every moment of
it with unalloyed joy. As I have said, these random
memoirs are to some extent autobiographical, perhaps I
may be allowed to describe my own situation. I had just
passed responsions and was due to go up to Oxford in
the autumn and, in those comparatively easy times, had a
summer before me without anything on my mind but a burning ambition to establish myself as a regular member of
the Middlesex side.

Nominally, Frank Mann was still captain of Middlesex
but, owing to business matters, he was unable to play in
the early matches. He was succeeded by Nigel Haig who
proved himself to be a most able captain. Throughout his
playing days he was one of the great personalities of the
cricket world. Tall and exceedingly spare, he was an all
round athlete, and had played ice hockey, real tennis, golf,
soccer, rugger and a variety of other games all to a high
standard. He had a witty and active mind, with interests
ranging from bird watching to music and poetry. He was
a wonderful companion and guide to us youngsters, and he
had a hot Scots temper which kept us, very properly, in
some awe of him. If I describe him in the past tense
it is because I am concerned with a specific period for I
should add that, at the age of 72, he retains all these qualities and when we meet or correspond it is always in the
the same unchanging vein.

In the early matches I continued to bowl quickish
medium, but was still bothered by lack of timing and co-
ordination. Against Yorkshire I launched forth as a fastish
seamer and, aided by ideal conditions, had a very good
match. In one spell on a real green Lord's wicket, I had
Wilfred Rhodes caught behind, knocked Emmott Robin-

59

son's castle down first ball, hit Maurice Leyland's off-stump without removing a bail and struck Herbert Sutcliffe's right leg so often that I nearly succeeded in removing that. Herbert was the doughtiest of opponents but, not inconsistently, a generous one, and he went out of his way to come and say "well bowled" at the end of the innings. But I was sure that I was never going to be a world-beater as a seamer.

The major change in my methods and prospects came when we played Leicester at Leicester. After a very unsuccessful first innings I cut my run in half and started to give the ball lots of air. The effect was immediate. I got six wickets in the second innings, went on to Worcester and got another six and generally began to enjoy myself to the full. Middlesex were a wonderfully handy bowling side whatever their quality. Haig and Durston with the new ball, and Robins and myself to spin with occasional auxiliaries for time of crisis. Haig managed his bowling most adroitly and always co-operated with the man in action. He reckoned he could always get a wicket out of us by signalling "one more over". By the end of the season he, Walter and myself had all taken 100 wickets which I believe is still a record amongst the counties where amateurs are concerned.

Every cricketer's age is probably the golden one in his eyes, but there are good grounds for claiming that the late 'twenties and early 'thirties was a particularly good era. To lend it depth and dignity there was still a fair sprinkling of the pre-first-war players active, and some who had been household names in Edwardian days. Middlesex boasted a splendid example of the latter school in Jack Hearne, variously and affectionately known as "J.W.," "Young Jack," or "Nutty". He was a great cricketer in every sense. Brought up in the impeccable traditions observed by his uncle, J. T. Hearne and Sir Pelham Warner, he was a great man for his team, never flagging until the match was won or lost, and never shirking an unpopular role. His batting had the same air of polish and restraint as his immaculate appearance which had earned him the last of the soubriquets I have quoted. His play was chiefly from the back foot, and he steered and pushed the ball rather than punched. But there was a day at Bradford once when he was a bit off colour, his health always being rather frail, and he went mad and lashed Verity and Macaulay all over the field. Curiously enough I can recall another particularly brilliant innings he played when far from well.

He has always been a most abstemious man, and a very modest evening would have a severely adverse effect on his rather delicate constitution the following day. One evening in Nottingham he was drawn, against his better judgement, into a card game with several of the tougher members of both sides. It developed into a real night amongst the harder cases and, although "J.W." gave up long before the end, we found him next morning in a state of approaching suspended animation. However, he was not out and determined to bat, although no-one gave much for his chances against Larwood and Voce.

With ashen face and unseeing eyes he set out for the middle with Pat Hendren as his partner. That impish man could never resist a little harmless fun, so nudged and guided the invalid to the centre of the ground, which was a considerable distance from the match which was taking place at one side. Poor "J.W.", looking bleakly about him, was under the impression that they had preceded the fielding side, but Pat, having had his jest, then escorted him to the scene proper. The state of affairs was now apparent to the opposition, and "J.W." confessed to Lol Larwood that he wasn't quite himself, and hinted that he would be grateful if Lol would pitch them up.

While this was going on, the succeeding batsman was pulling on his gloves in anticipation of the immediate fall of a wicket. He, with everyone else, was confounded and astonished. The batsman, possibly animated by a temporary and uncharacteristic hatred of the world at large, fairly let fly and before the bowlers realised what had happened he had flogged them for forty most brilliant runs. At that point it seemed he was overwhelmed by a wave of nausea, for he made a vicious square cut several feet above a straight half-volley and was castled utterly. The only other incident of the day I recall was accompanying him to visit another invalid in the afternoon. The casualty in this case was George Gunn who had contracted simultaneously the two most incompatible complaints in the entire book, namely arthritis and dysentery. I shall never forget how the sufferer laughed in describing his predicament.

Somehow this was in pattern with George Gunn's whole career, which was original and entertaining beyond that of any other of the major batsmen. Of his majestically temperamental batting almost everything has been written and said, but just the other day a new item came to my hearing. Claude Taylor recalled that once at Leicester, when it seemed that time hung heavy on the great man's hands, he turned to the slips and invited their suggestions as to what stroke he should play to the next ball bowled. They, entering into the spirit of the thing, made all sorts of extravagant requests, which the virtuoso faithfully carried out with a large degree of success.

Of his interests outside the game of cricket, he was a fine pianist, having had early ambitions to be a professional accompanist, but abandoning this career on discovering where his real genius lay. One scene has always lived in my memory since I heard it described by Nigel Haig in whose home it occurred. Occasionally assisted by his audience consisting of Nigel and Nigel's mother (incidentally a very remarkable and charming old lady), George played and sang his way through the score of "Tom Jones". The evening was a most notable success.

For Pat Hendren the season of 1929 was a very variable one. Despite a very successful tour of Australia he ran into a rut of bad luck early on and could not get started. The climax in his misfortunes arose when we played Nottinghamshire at Lord's and he was out to Sam Staples in the most extraordinary way. An off-break pitched so wide that it dropped in a bowler's imprint on the neighbouring wicket. From this it shot back at a steep angle, and hit the end of the bat handle like a billiard cue, and shot into the stumps. This was too much and Hendren, seeing the fates against him, determined to have a bang again. This proved the right answer and he was soon himself again. Some years later when Don Bradman was out of form he appealed to Pat at first slip for advice and was advised to follow the same course. The results were disastrous from the fielding side's point of view from that moment onwards.

Amongst the great batsmen of all time Hendren must have a secure place. He was a fine player of every type of bowling, fast of foot against spin, and strong and resolute against the quicks. He was a magnificent hooker, and few fast bowlers bounced him a second time. He would station himself exactly in line with the ball, and so could place his stroke precisely within a fairly large sector as he gave it a full-blooded thump from his immensely strong wrists and forearms. Apart from his prowess as a player he had a personality which appealed to every crowd beyond any other cricketer of my time. He is still affectionately remembered all over Australia and was received with something approaching delirium in the West Indies, where babies, buses and boats were christened Patsy by the score.

The first year of the 'thirties saw the retirement of Jack Hobbs from Test Match cricket where, as in every other sphere of the game, he had established a position and reputation unchallenged in the minds of those who saw and played with him. There may have been more spectacular players and more voracious run-getters, but I never saw another batsman who was so sufficient against every type of bowling and on every type of pitch.

By 1930 responsibility and prudence had tempered his earlier impetuosity, but he retained this dominating quality. He did what was required without fuss or frills. It was only when a struggling partner so woefully failed to do what was needed that one was aware of the difficulties and the deceptive ease of perfection. The same might be said of his fielding at cover point where, with all his speed and accuracy, there was never a hint of bustle.

It was my good luck to play with and against " the Master " a number of times, and I once even got him out (on the only occasion I missed his bat). If the very young players regarded him with some awe, it was on account of his position; for, in his greatness, he was thoughtful and kind enough to give at least one young bowler a special word of encouragement as he prepared to bowl a first nervous ball against Australia. It was in after years that I personally got to know him and appreciate his zest for life, and the wonderful sense of fun which keeps him so youthful and sprightly.

In the same year, Wilfred Rhodes retired from county cricket, and so was broken one of the longest links in the game. If cricket was to him a sort of secondary religion, he was the greatest theologian of his time, and I remember Greville Stevens saying to me that, having played for England, he imagined he knew quite a bit about the game until he went on tour with Wilfred and heard him expatiate.

These, then, were the grand vintage, the majority of whom had contributed to the great days of Foster and Barnes. All had done their best to speed the re-establishment of English cricket in the lean days of the early 1920s and, now in the ripe old age of their cricketing days, added much grace and charm to the scene in addition to a wealth of material skill.

The 'twenties, after much toil and travail, had produced a splendid school of both batsmen and bowlers, who were either in their prime or still going strong. Perhaps the eve of the 'thirties saw this blend of power and experience at its best under Percy Chapman in Australia, when it overwhelmed a home side in a somewhat uncertain and transitory state.

Chapman may not have been the greatest of England captains, judged as a tactician or player, but he was certainly the most popular. He also caught the public imagination, as did Hendren, if in a very different way.

Large, cherubic and debonair, there was a golden touch about his cricket which illuminated every stage of it. He had been promoted captain of England when his predecessor, Arthur Carr, had fallen from grace, and at one stroke recaptured the Ashes, beyond our grasp these many years. It was a sad irony that this primrose path ended, as it had begun, with a change of captain while the series was in progress.

Hammond was undoubtedly the greatest cricketer of this school, being a fine seam bowler in addition to his batting and fielding. His final place among the immortals, however, is hard to judge. A phenomenal series against Australia in 1928-29 was followed by a number of comparatively lean ones until, as captain, he burst forth with his superb 240 when, at Lord's in 1938, Ernie McCormick had routed the first three English batsmen.

This less productive period was in some measure due to the fact that, while he was absolutely supreme on the off side, he was much less powerful on the on, and the Australians, headed by O'Reilly, once they had grasped the situation, concentrated on his leg stump.

His power in county cricket was tremendous. In his early days, when Gloucester had a number of somewhat uncertain, if deliberate, fielders, it was said that, whenever the ball was hit as high as a telegraph pole, a chorus of "Yours, Wally" arose, regardless of his position at the moment.

Yorkshire were the leading county throughout the 'thirties and almost certainly the best led. Brian Sellers is most thoroughly a Yorkshireman, and has a great and instinctive knowledge of his fellow tykes. He handled his team with a firm but understanding hand. England players or novices, he encouraged, castigated, exhorted, congratulated, cursed or flayed them without ceremony or distinction, all in the vernacular, and with a flow of lurid and picturesque metaphor, calculated to touch the subject's heart or nerve centres, as required, and fill the casual hearer with awe. He knew exactly when to drive and when to lead, with the result that his team was a wonderfully close-knit and efficient unit.

I have written of Holmes and Sutcliffe, but of all the great characters who played for Yorkshire none has left a happier legend than Maurice Leyland. His bat was as broad as his beam and he loved a battle, which he always conducted in the best possible humour with ever a jest, the keener and drier because it was delivered in slow Yorkshire tones.

When, in Australia, his colleagues voiced fears of O'Reilly, Maurice stated in matter-of-fact tones that he thought he had O'Reilly " skinned to death ". When he returned with a century under his belt his captain, G. O. Allen, gratefully acknowledged that he had been as good as his word. " Aye ", said the grinning striker, " and I'll tell you summat else—now he knows it."

The greatest and most controversial bowler of the age was, of course, Harold Larwood. He led a group of fine fast bowlers in the late 'twenties and early 'thirties but was alone in his perfection. He may have had his equals in other periods but few of his contemporaries will believe he has had or will have a superior.

For the younger who want some impression of his action I would say, picture Lindwall at his best with an arm that came right over the top and a swing so great that he occasionally rapped his knuckles on the wicket. Douglas Jardine used to say he could judge the amount of effort Larwood was exerting in any particular spell by the vigour with which he brushed his dusty fist on his shirt as he walked back. It is at least a very picturesque legend.

Larwood may have been conquered on the lifeless wickets of the 1930 series, but he took a fearsome revenge two years later. Whether he would have been so successful without the leg-side field will always be a matter of controversy.

Maurice Tate was on the decline by the start of the

'thirties but still had his great moments. When, for once in a way, he got a green wicket to operate on he bowled out six of the superb 1930 Australian batting side for eighteen at Hove. Those who played maintain that he had Alan Kippax caught at the wicket for nought, but that dashing and gallant player of strokes once more had the luck attributed to his kind, and used it to make 100 and so transform the situation.

There was, in addition to Larwood and Tate, a fine band of fast bowlers. Allen was a magnificent bowler of beautiful action and great pace. His worth was questioned after a solitary appearance in the series of 1930 when he met Bradman and company on an impossibly good wicket at Lord's; but this was wholly unjust. It was a proposition which defeated Larwood and would have baffled McDonald, Lindwall, Lockwood or Alfred Mynn himself. Two years later he was given a fairer chance in Australia, and immediately showed his true quality in the highest class. Voce was just coming up as a fast left hander, and was closely rivalled by Clark of Northants., whose shortcomings were suspected to be more temperamental than technical. Bowes used his enormous height and the new ball to best advantage and was, when fully developed, the most consistent of the fastish seam division. Verity, White, Robins, Freeman, Goddard, Clay and Tyldesley led the slow bowlers, while Geary and Macaulay cut and spun the ball at a sharp pace. Duckworth and Ames were sufficiently talented behind the stumps to make a choice between them something of an embarrassment to the selectors, but eventually Ames' batting carried the day.

As Australia had lost the two previous series, the immediate prior one by a crushing margin, the arrival of the 1930 team was received with something approaching complacency. This was disturbed at an early stage in the tour, and shattered before it was over. The chief shattering agent was of course Bradman who, on the pluperfect wickets of that era, displayed a sustained power of stroke unequalled before or since. But the supporting Australian batting was of such calibre that it is arguable that the first half of the order was the best that Australia has ever put in the field. It was led by the rock-like defence of Woodfull, "the unbowlable", who was supported by Ponsford, a magnificent technician and the most fully equipped Australian batsman to come to England in my time. A massive start usually smoothed the way for a devastating onslaught by Bradman and, with the tide flowing, there was the graceful stroke play of Kippax to maintain the flow. McCabe must go very high amongst Australian batsmen of all time. He was a particularly good player of fast bowling, better than either Bradman or Ponsford, and a most able player of any other type. The main weight of the batting was completed by Vic Richardson, a rough, tough, cheerful and dangerous performer; but if things did go wrong Fairfax would prod away with endless patience, as Kelleway had done before him. The tragedy of 1930 was the ill-health of Archie Jackson, born in Scotland and hailed in his adopted country as the new Victor Trumper. Had he lived up to the hopes of his supporters he would have been the greatest of the lot, and the imagination wilts at the picture of this batting side on the pitches provided for it. In fact Jackson was a sick man though always game, and he was further handicapped by persistent bad luck in the early matches.

Observers were inclined to caption the Australian bowling of 1930 as "Grimmett and Friends" but this was not entirely true. Fairfax was a better quick medium bowler than any other Australian to come here since the first war, and got some very valuable wickets. He had the unique distinction of ending Jack Hobbs' Test Match career, but was a bit lucky in that the master cut the ball into his wicket. Tim Wall was not of the really fast, but persistent and accurate at all times, and dangerous when the ball would move. The others had little success but good fielding and Bert Oldfield behind the wicket made for very adequate out-cricket.

The New Zealanders brought a world class batsman in

Dempster and a very good one in Page in addition to a fine all-rounder in Blunt when they came in '31. In 1932 All India were seen as a touring Test Match side for the first time. Their best feature was a fine pair of opening bowlers in Nissar and Amar Singh. Nissar was a good straight-forward fast bowler of fine physique, but rather square on action, who bowled his best on the big occasion. Amar Singh was an altogether exceptional cricketer. He was a tall beautifully built man with a feline grace and smoothness of movement. He ran about half-a-dozen short, tripping steps and bowled fastish, with a quick whip-like action which gave him a great life and lift from the pitch. He could do the usual seam bowler's tricks with the new ball, but in addition could impart a certain amount of spin by cutting the ball, a talent which made him a very good bowler on damaged or matting wickets. He fielded with the same lithe agility and, on occasions, hit with great effect. He was much the most interesting Indian cricketer to visit this country with the possible exception of Vinoo Mankad and a great draw when he went to a Northern league club.

These two were supported by Jahangir Khan, a fine strong young man who bowled fast medium with a lowish action, and later got a blue at Cambridge. While an undergraduate he performed a unique if unintended feat, by picking off a sparrow while bowling at Tom Pearce at Lord's. Bird and ball arrived together at the batsman's feet, but fortunately neither hit the wicket to disturb the bails and the umpire's peace of mind. The bird is now stuffed and sits a-top of the ball under a glass case in the Long Room.

In 1933 the West Indies came again bringing the quick-silver Constantine once again and two notable new-comers. Martindale was a bounding fast bowler, with a curious, rather stumbling run and a beautiful wheeling action. With Constantine he rather turned the tables on Douglas Jardine by bowling bouncers to a "body-line" field, a counter-assault which the inventor received with rock-like defiance. George Headley turned out to be the best coloured batsman the West Indies had yet produced. He was popularly known as "The Black Bradman" but he was in fact a very different type of player, and lacked Bradman's enormous power, preferring the back foot, upon which he defended beautifully, and from which he played a great variety of neat scoring strokes.

The Australian series of 1934 was notable in that for the first and only time the great spinning combination of O'Reilly and Grimmett operated in this country. Of all slow bowling duets I have seen it was the tops by a fair margin. The two partners might have been specifically designed for each other and the job in hand. They were alike in the essentials of extreme accuracy and subtlety of flight, but in tactical detail very different yet complementary. O'Reilly was really a medium pacer who rolled the leg-break a shade, and spun the top-spinner and googly sharply. Grimmett spun and flighted the leg-break at a slow pace and used the quicker top-spinner as an offensive variant. His googly was more an agent of propaganda than destruction.

England scored heavily against this formidable attack on perfect wickets but no side made any great headway, once the surface gave any bite in the shape of dust or wet. Had they bowled at their best on the English pitches of 1956 the batsmen would have had a very thin time indeed.

In support of the main battery there came "Chuck" Fleetwood-Smith, the first really notable left-handed googly bowler. He spun the ball prodigiously, more than anyone but Arthur Mailey. He was also on the quick side for this type of bowler but, apart from these extraordinary talents, he lacked the control and craft of the other two. He was nonetheless always an acute danger and, characteristically, ensured Australian victory in a series with one ball. It was the perfect left-hander's off-break which bowled Wally Hammond neck and crop at Adelaide in 1936. On his bad days he could, like the little girl of the rhyme, be horrid, and in his last Test Match returned the spectacular figures of one for 298.

The series was well contested, for England had some up-and-coming young men as well as some pretty good old 'uns; but just about the mid-'thirties there was a slight recession while one generation succeeded another. Hobbs, Sutcliffe, Larwood, Tate, Jardine were giving way to Barnett, Hutton, Compton, Farnes, Wright and Edrich. As a result of this slight hiatus a very good South African team won a series in England for the first time in 1935. And because of its obvious shortcomings the M.C.C. side sailing for Australia a year later was given little or no chance of victory by the prophets. These wiseacres were confounded by Allen's happy combination of good luck and good leadership, and had not the former deserted at the most critical moment, they would have had to eat their words most utterly.

It may be said, therefore, that the 'thirties could be divided into two clear halves in terms of English cricket as well as time. The dividing point is just about that at which the LBW law was experimentally introduced; but this is largely coincidental for the effect of this change on batsmanship was not immediately apparent. By 1937 the younger generation was asserting itself and the next year England were a very good side indeed. The probability is that had the game gone on uninterrupted for another few years English cricket would have developed its greatest possible strength. All the young stars were robbed of six of their brightest years which, carried along by the momentum of progress, would have gone to make a wonderful period. Besides this immense loss there is the incalculable factor of the talent which never came to light in these six years, when cricket training and coaching was a very unimportant matter.

The cricket of the 'thirties differed from both that of the 'twenties and that of the post-war times. Bradman, doped wickets and four-day Test Matches brought about a minor revolution in international cricket which had as a sequel the so-called " body-line " attack eighteen months later. The connexion between the revolution of 1930 and the reaction of 1932-3 is not difficult to see. The domination of bat over ball, and the stultifying of the bowler on overprepared wickets together with the match-winning supremacy of Bradman attracted attention and reprisals. Leg theory provoked, in its turn, a furore, and for the next few seasons fast bowlers had to be very chary about the combination of bouncer and leg-side field. These events no doubt hastened the introduction of the alteration to the LBW law which has, in the course of time, had a very considerable effect on the character of the game.

Its immediate effect on stroke play was not so very great. Human beings accustomed to a certain set of circumstances in their formative years do not readily lose characteristics and outlook which have become instinctive. This is naturally also true of cricketers. The free swinging Dominion batsman who has acquired his style on fast, smooth surfaces has much difficulty curbing his stroke when he gets on a wet English wicket, where the ball checks on pitching. Many English players have known what alterations have been necessary to adapt their methods to the pace and bounce of Australian wickets, but have failed to combat the inborn habits of years. In the broader aspect the batsman who had been brought up to play strokes to the off did not completely abandon them in the face of this new threat. The bowler, also still habit bound, scarcely altered his method of attacking the off stump, but looked forward to collecting the just rewards of beating the bat. Thus, with good wickets prevailing for the most part, the late 'thirties continued to produce attractive cricket. Hutton, Compton, Barnett and Edrich were all eager stroke players in their youth, and there were some notable hitters such as Smith (J.), Bartlett and Wellard. I would not include in this attraction England's enormous score at the Oval in 1938 on, once again, a wicket upon which bowlers abandoned all hope almost before entering.

The great point was that play was chiefly to the off and the spirit was to get on with the game rather than save it from the word "go". There was much less deliberate slowing of the tempo and, amongst other details, fast bowlers seemed to run a reasonable distance. Larwood, Allen, Bowes, Voce and the like ran about twelve to seventeen yards and could get rid of an over in smart time. Wall and McCormick both ran about twenty-five yards, but seldom if ever did one see two long-distance performers in action together, and never up to four in a team. The spinners bowled much as to-day, for it is a mistake to think that the off-spinner to a close leg-side field with the deep well guarded is a post-war invention. What is true is that the off-spinner of the 'thirties only occasionally had the opportunity to bowl on the dusty wickets which in certain places in the 'fifties became almost standard practice. And the dusty wicket is generally a better bet than rain for the spinner, as only a real sticky one can equal it for pace and bounce.

On the international plane England ended the 'thirties on a rising note of great strength, with Australia and South Africa relatively keeping pace. The West Indies had not achieved their post-war power but were a great attraction. The lesser powers toured this country very happily and, with three Test Matches of three days each, did nothing to interfere with the domestic programme.

The county scene was, of course, dominated by a powerful Yorkshire who provided purposeful but fascinating cricket. Middlesex, under Walter Robins, were always on their toes with win or lose as their watchword. Perhaps the greatest drawback to county cricket in the 'thirties was that the humbler counties had little prospect of bettering their lot in the lower half of the table. In the absence of Supporters' Clubs the very necessary artificial financial respiration came chiefly from loyal and affluent patrons, but this gave little scope for development. Some of them were, nonetheless, rather jolly institutions and it is gratifying that many, having stuck it out, have prospered greatly in after years.

It was all in all a very happy time to be interested in cricket, actively or otherwise.

73

CHAPTER NINE

Rest Cure

AUTHOR'S NOTE. This, I need hardly say, is a true story, but, as is sometimes necessary in circumstances of delicacy and dramatic force, names of people and places have been disguised in order to spare pain and embarrassment to anyone concerned still showing occasional signs of animation.

MY OLD FRIEND OLIVER BASSOON, BEING A GOOD all-rounder in his varsity days, got a " blue " in his last year. He had the edge on most all-rounders, however, in that he came down with a serviceable degree which immediately led to a post in a firm of solicitors. There, on payment of a reasonable premium, he was privileged to work like a beaver, thus enabling his superiors to enjoy an occasional day's golf or fishing. Always a conscientious man, at the end of a couple of years he had so given of his best that he was nigh to nervous exhaustion. Happily at that critical moment he received an invitation to accompany a cricket team on a short tour of Egypt.

His boss, a kindly man for a solicitor, thought it a good idea that he should go, especially when he reflected that he had about drained the last drop of blood, and the premium for the current year had been fully paid up.

" You're looking a bit tired," he said, " although I can't think why. This will set you up and you can put in a bit of extra time when you get back."

As he packed his traps on the eve of the expedition Oliver's hands trembled as much from anticipation as from exhaustion. He had no time for cricket in the ordinary way, and the prospect of starting again in the warm oriental sun was enchanting. Besides, at heart he was young and romantic, and the glamour and gaiety of the life before him was strangely exciting, after the incessant grind of the past two years. He made doubly sure of catching the train the following morn, and was first of the team on the platform but one.

The one was a pretty big "but".

The Bimbashi, who was there to greet him, was a man of commanding aspect. His air of authority was accentuated by a club foot due, so contemporaries averred, to his toes being trodden on by a public-spirited elephant. He greeted his young team-mate with genial condescension, and proposed a turn up and down the platform while they waited.

"What's your name, young fellah?" he demanded, after a few pleasantries about the weather and the deplorable state of the country.

"Bassoon, sir", said Oliver.

"Eh? What? Well, indeed", said the Bimbashi, with great cordiality, "Why, bless my soul, I knew old Snuffy Babboon of the 133rd like a brother. Well, well", he said, "We'll share a cabin."

Oliver says that, had he been in any sort of shape, he could have put a stop to this preposterous situation there and then. But by the time he had marshalled his bemused senses the Bimbashi was off again, extolling the virtues of old Snuffy on safari. It was clearly expected that any other member of the family would live up to them, and before the last of the team had arrived the relationship had been fully established, the shackles secured and the branding iron applied. Oliver was introduced to several of his oldest cronies with proprietorial pride as "my young friend Babboon Heah" and dismayed when they further complicated the issue by gleefully addressing him by this distortion of his proper name.

As we travelled pleasantly overland to Genoa Oliver's duties were comparatively light; a bit of fetching and carrying and seeing the baggage through the Customs. Things went pretty smoothly, although he did get a bit of a wigging for giving a porter a couple of francs more than his master, not a man to pamper servants, had authorised. This, however, he described as a pin-prick compared to the fluent gallic estimate of his character and parentage he got from the recipient.

On board ship the routine was tightened up, and once on land got into its full stride. The day started for Oliver at 0600 hours with a cold sponge applied to his heavily slumbering face. Instantly and dismally he crawled out of bed to polish up the brass boot and secure it to its owner's foot. Having attended to the details of his master's toilet he dressed feverishly to take advantage of "the best part of the day". At first he looked forward to the early morning's net practice; but this turned out to be a prolonged bowl at the Bimbashi who prescribed every delivery to be bowled.—"One to cut", "an over to leg", "dammit, sir, don't you know what a yorker is?" As the Egyptian sun bore down ever more fiercely and his colleagues abandoned their gentle exertions for the delights of the swimming pool, Oliver hastily collected a bundle of reference books before being marched off to some improving centre.

When the matches started it was apparent that Bassoon was going to take a very active part in the proceedings. The Bimbashi was a fine player, and his scuffle with the elephant had done nothing to diminish his powers of stroke. On the other hand, it did necessitate the services of a runner. Oliver has often told me in after days that it was not so much the physical effort of running upwards of 800 runs in a temperature of 120 in the shade which told on him, but the nervous strain of being roundly cursed every time he ran, or violently abused every time he did not.

His really strenuous time was in the field. The Bimbashi liked to stand at mid-off where, being immobile, he was only effective to the direct hit. However, he was a considerate man and, realising that he might cause his captain some embarrassment, he made arrangements to alleviate any difficulty. Bassoon was stationed behind him at long-off, both ends. There he was fully employed and closely supervised on the hard, fast outfield during overs, at the end of which he set out on his long gallop to the further end of the arena. His painful progress through the gauntlet of the inner field was enlivened by good-natured chaff from the mid-off such as "Come along slow coach" or "Pick 'em up there, Stiffy."

A few overs from time to time afforded him some physical relaxation, if occasionally adding to the emotional strain. As when the batsman skied the ball between the bowler and mid-off and the Bimbashi took charge of the situation with a deafening cry of "Mine". The ball snicked the brim of his topee with a sharp tutting sound before falling heavily at his feet. Oliver's mumbled expressions of sympathy were cut short when the ball was shot back at him with a snake-like flip of the wrist, ankle high. As, owing to the general wear and tear on his legs, he had abandoned the encumbrance of boots and socks for the lighter "sneaker", the ball caught him an agonising crack on his unprotected joint. In the frenzy of his gyrations the directive, to bowl properly as he would never get them out with "that tosh", was lost, but for some days after his gait closely resembled that of his master. He was not, of course, excused duty on that account.

Off the field the festivities were such that it was afterwards said (without foundation in fact) that I alone of the side enjoyed a night's rest, having fallen asleep on a tram and gone to the depot. But this could not have been true, if I had in fact boarded a tram, for Bassoon at least got to bed early. Nightly, as the clock struck ten and the wine flowed free, the music swelled, the magic veil of the Nile was cleft asunder by a great booming cry of "Babboooon!"

It affected Oliver as the bay of the Hound a tenant of Baskerville Hall—"time we were gettin' home, young fellah." An embarrassed hostess having refused generous offers of his assistance in the servants' quarters, he was genially driven into the night.

This final humiliation probably saved his health and he lasted the course remarkably well, finishing only slightly thinner and more careworn than he started.

Were this not a true story I would have been tempted to give it a happy ending of the faithful-service-rewarded type. Unfortunately, in truth this beautiful friendship came to a sad and sudden end on the last lap, in the train for Victoria. Having seen the baggage through the Customs, Oliver sank into the seat opposite his master. The Bimbashi was in capital form, bright purple from the Egyptian sun and the English frost. He was thumbing through the clippings of the tour which Oliver had kept for him.

"These press wallahs," he laughed. "Same the world over. Got your name wrong every time—call you Bassoon. Ha Ha."

"That happens to be my name," said Oliver in a palely mutinous voice.

"Bassoon?" The Bimbashi's formidable features were a rectangle of suspicion and affront. "Are ye tellin' me that you're no relation of old Snuffy Babboon?"

"No, I am not", replied Oliver—and "Glory be " he added with a fine defiance.

The Bimbashi breathed heavily and, running his eye over his hand baggage, made an obvious mental note to check its contents at the first opportunity. He opened his mouth as if to speak and then, with a grinding of the teeth, raised his paper and spoke no more. At Victoria he said "Goodbye—er—Basssssoon." With a fierce sarcasm of the sybilants hissing in his ears Oliver sped arrow-like to the office.

"Well", said his boss, "after six weeks loaf you'll feel like a bit of work again."

Oliver's heart went out to him. Beneath a skyscraper of files he staggered to his desk and carved in. Perhaps that is why he is now head of the firm.

He came round for a drink the other night and, apart from verbally corroborating these few details I have set down, endorsed them by two persistent characteristics. The first is, like another customer of Sherlock Holmes, he has a strong aversion to limping men. The second is something of a social asset. On introduction he enunciates his name slowly and clearly to the stranger and, in cases of doubt, spells it at dictation speed.

CHAPTER TEN

The Good Antipodean Earth

IF, WHEN IN AUSTRALIA, YOU ASK AN Australian friend how your cricket team is doing and he replies that, at stumps, they were two for nine, and adds that he has just left the Oval, do not panic. He means that at the close of play your team has lost two wickets in making nine runs—*not*, as you might suppose, made two runs and lost nine wickets. Nor has he, through sun or excitement, fallen prey to delusion that he has been to Kennington. In Australia all cricket grounds are Ovals, and are tended not by groundsmen but by curators. Wonderful cricket grounds they are too.

The M.C.C. now invariably kicks off at Perth, which boasts a vast playing area and, on occasions, the fastest wicket in Australia. There is also plenty of space around, but the stand accommodation is considerably less than that of rival centres, which is at times a sensitive point. For many of the citizens think the time is ripe when Perth should have a Test Match, instead of Sydney and Melbourne being given a second in alternate series. This naturally meets with some brisk opposition in these quarters, but it is a question on which the visiting fireman is well advised to say nowt. At least by listening he learns some interesting things, such as the fact that Perth is separated from the next city by a greater distance than is any comparable community on earth. This, needless to say, has a different significance for each side in the argument.

The distant but next-door neighbour is, of course, Adelaide, where is enthroned the Queen, or certainly the Beauty Queen, of Australian cricket grounds. The area itself is most comely, with its trim grey red-roofed stands flanked by green banks and trees. The Cathedral, standing on a hill to the West, may be obscured from certain parts of the members' stand by the large and highly efficient score board; but if the spectator raises his eye from the play it travels over the lush, almost sub-tropical, vegetation, to the gracious line of the Mount Lofty Range, fifteen miles away. If he be a Celt, his soul may well wing onwards another twelve thousand miles to the hills of Strathmore, which the Mount Lofties so closely resemble.

If you have a taste for the straight drive you had best take in your heaviest bat at Adelaide, for the distance between the screens is about two hundred and eight yards. It used to be longer when a cycling track surrounded the turf. Once when I stood on this ground a most knowledgeable Adelaidian pointed to a bench just behind the rails saying that it marked an historic spot. Long ago, in 1901, Clem Hill, fresh from his ninety-nine in the Melbourne Test, had reached ninety-eight on this ground when he struck Braund so high and far that Johnny Tyldesley, at long on, was forced on to the track where he made the catch. Seeing the batsman departing, this ever fair-minded Lancastrian ran towards him, shouting that he had caught it on the track so it could not be out. When within earshot he received a grateful, if torrid, reply to the effect that the track was within the legal area. Some will remember that Hill got ninety-seven in the second innings, so might, with some justification, have thought himself a bit hardly done by all round.

The approach to the Melbourne cricket ground is also one of great beauty. The traveller can walk through the park with its trees and grass, and exquisite masses of flowers and colour. He may even pause at Captain Cook's cottage (transported and rebuilt brick by brick) to pay homage. His first view of the ground will be in somewhat striking contrast to this pastoral scene.

Melbourne is a vast amphitheatre surrounding and almost overpowering a huge circular playing area. In deference to police requirements the accommodation is limited to 105,000, but the magnificent new stand alone seats 43,000 people, or rather more than any English ground can take when jam packed. In the old days the playing field dropped as much as nine feet from end to end, so that Ray Lindwall would always prefer to bowl downhill, whatever the position of the wind. The major works carried out in preparation for the 1956 Olympic Games have reduced the drop to four feet, so the problem is now eased. The effect of this upheaval on the wicket seems to be but slight.

Comparisons are perhaps more than ever odious when drawn by a guest, but it is only honest to say that many who have played on it consider Sydney the best *cricket* ground in Australia, maybe in the world. It has all the qualities that go to make good cricket—a perfect wicket, beautiful light, a spacious and smooth outfield and first class accommodation. Not least, it boasts the Hill, the spiritual home of all barrackers. There is every amenity for the player, including an adjacent and full-sized practice ground on which many of Australia's greatest have first shown their youthful paces in the hopes of impressing the critics. It was here that a distinguished panel were mildly amused by the bucolic unorthodoxy of a young man from Bowral, named Bradman. Their mood was tempered to one of reflection when Arthur Mailey pointed out that, after ten minutes' play, no ball bowled had reached the back of the net.

Brisbane differs from these other grounds in that it is the most Northern, and being sub-tropical, the vegetation and climate are rather more exotic. When it rains in earnest it doesn't matter awfully whether the groundsman gets there in time with the covers or not, for in a very few minutes they can be floating around on a respectable depth of water. This is of course unusual, and for the most part it is a green and perfect wicket.

At one time the accommodation for the players was, to say the least of it, hardly adequate but, just before the arrival of Peter May's team, extensive alterations and additions were made to the pavilion. It is now most up to date, and houses a first class press box.

Brisbane, according to non-Queenslanders, has something of a reputation for adventure and mis-adventure. When May's team played the State we had a mild edition of the tropical showers I have described, and the staff rushed out with a promptitude which would have done credit to the London Fire Brigade (although they are admittedly bodies devoted to diametrically opposed purposes). The covers were down in record time and presently the rain stopped. The sun shone and everything was lovely except for a large marshy patch in the most vital place where the covers had leaked. Because of this no further play was possible, and the crowd gathered round the splendid pavilion and vented their feelings on the management. An announcement was made that free passes would be issued for the morrow, but this merely led to a volley of suggestions, some original, some conspicuously less so, as to what the management could do with their passes.

Viewing this scene, a Victorian waggled his head and sighed "There's always something at Brisbane." He said he could remember the days when they had a horse roller and, between innings in one match, lost the horse. Apart from the embarrassment caused to the hosts, this would seem to raise a rather tricky legal situation, but, possibly to avoid future complication, the wayward beast was replaced by a steam roller. This, according to my friend, proved to be even more temperamental for at least the horse, when located, could be persuaded to perform at the required moment, which was not always so in the case of its mechanical successor. Owing to some defect of design or construction the manipulation of this contrivance called for delicate timing. If stoked up too soon it was liable to blow up, and if the process was too long delayed there was never enough steam to get under way. Thus the curator would watch the later batsmen in an agony of speculation as to whether an unexpected collapse would catch him with pressure gauge at half mast, or an inconvenient last wicket stand precipitate an explosion. However, time marches and there is now a splendid diesel machine and, anyway, as I have said, my informant was a Victorian. For my money Brisbane is a pleasant place in early summer before the thermometer gets substantially over the hundred mark.

As one whose knowledge of grass is limited to the fact that it is green and, inconveniently, needs cutting once a week, I was interested to learn something of the physical characteristics of those grounds from an expert, Mr. Watt, who recently left the Sydney ground to re-establish the Melbourne turf. The grass used on all is couch (pronounced kootch, as the proper name for a sofa in Scotland). It thrives on sun and constant cutting produces a very fine texture. Each ground has its own subsoil brought from neighbouring districts, Bulli at Sydney, Merri Creek at Melbourne and Athelstone at Adelaide, and it is laid on the table to a considerable depth — eighteen inches at Sydney. Even so, Australian pitches generally seem to suffer from the same creeping malady as our own. They seem to grow progressively slower. Would geologists or botanists, or both, combine to find the explanation and supply the answer? It is very important to the future of cricket.

CHAPTER ELEVEN

T'Lane Revisited

CRICKET GROUNDS HAVE AS PRONOUNCED AND varied personalities as cricketers themselves. As in the case of the cricketer the personality of the ground is composed of a mass of ingredients—appearance, associations and nationality; but where cricket grounds are concerned the greatest factor is, of course, the people who have made it, played on it and who support it.

As Canterbury is characteristic of Kent, and the spirit of Surrey permeates the Oval, so Bramall Lane epitomises the soul of Yorkshire cricket, plain, blunt, determined, full of character. It is not beautiful but, apart from the great grounds kept prominently in the public eye by frequent Test Matches, it is possibly the best known of English cricket grounds. Like other persons or objects of special affection it is seldom given its full title by its intimates. Jack Stephenson, of fast medium swerve and Essex fame, eager to make his maiden appearance thereon, instructed the taxi man to bear him to *Bramall Lane* and was admonished. "T'Lane's enoof", said the charioteer.

Aye, t'Lane. But it was its full title which was originally stamped upon my imagination and engraved in my memory. Long years ago, Claude Taylor recounted to myself, and an equally enraptured brother, how, when representing his native county of Leicester he spent a day of murk and rain there, punctuated only by inspections of the wicket. The tea-time one proved final and the home captain made a reluctant signal to the few remaining spectators that all was over. At that, a window in t'Lane itself was thrown up and a great voice, hoarse with frustration, swelled out, "Dost tha think", it cried, "that Ah pays rent to stay in Bramall Lane for *this?*"

It is not really the place to speculate on the tragedy lying beyond that great cri de coeur, but it has haunted me ever since and, over the years, a clear picture has crystallised in my mind. He was, of course, a night worker roused from his fitful daylight slumbers by his wife — "Zachary, Zachary, wake oop—captains are out agin." Red-eyed but hopeful he leaps once more from his bed and, staggering to the window, is just in time to receive the final message of gloom. He throws up the sash and, such is human frailty, vents his exasperation upon the innocent bearer of ill tidings.

When the night worker uttered his cry of agony his district was, as now, one of plain, grim industry and smoke-begrimed brick and mortar. According to the illustrations of a very good booklet published for the Centenary, some years past, the ground was originally laid out in what was almost open country. The adjoining road got its name from the Brammall family, who made files and gravers, and lived in The White House at the corner. According to the text and further illustrations the whole venture was successfully floated in 1854, on a billowing ocean of spade beards.

The next twenty years saw the pastoral character of the district much changed, and by the 'eighties and 'nineties the surrounding prosperity was evident in the smog above and about. It used to be said that the stokers had always a few extra shovelfuls in hand for the over-successful visiting batsman. Sometimes, if one may say so, these patriots mis-fired. As when, with Yorkshire in the field, the safest catch in England was seen to station himself under a towering hit into the deep. His colleagues, as ever, regarded the striker's fate as surely sealed as though his middle stump lay flat on the ground, but were puzzled and dismayed to see the fielder hesitate, recover himself, falter and finally abandoning all effort, allow the ball to fall heavily at his feet. At the end of the over his captain testily demanded an explanation. "You see yon black patch", replied the culprit, indicating a wodge of smoke and fog directly over the pavilion. "Well I sees her go oop, and then she gits in black patch and I loses her. Then I sees her int sky, then she drops in black patch again, so I says bother and leaves her."

Commenting on this the other day a Sheffield lady said, rather primly, that Bramall Lane was going to be a smokeless zone, or at any rate the smoke was now no longer black, but yellow and very beautiful.

It is hoped that the colour scheme will in no way alter the character of the regulars who have for long been known for a fine mixture of feudalism, democracy, respect and outspokenness. Surely all these sterling qualities are perfectly illustrated in an old member's recollection of Lord Hawke serving a temporary, and unusual, spell in the deep. Some miscalculation led to the ball trickling through the nobleman's legs and thence over the line, a calamity which must have resembled a frivolous procession flowing beneath an august monumental arch. For this lapse he was roundly castigated by a neighbouring spectator in terms both plain and blunt. His lordship heard this rebuke to its end with simple dignity, then turned his imperious eye on the speaker. "Quite right, my man", he said, before setting out for some more familiar part of the field.

The Lanites (or Lanians) though kind of heart were never respecters of persons. When Charles Fry batted all day with Prince Ranjitsinhji he was periodically refreshed by a waiter with a glass on a silver tray. That his partner was on each occasion completely neglected struck one spectator (possibly irked by the repeated interruptions) as being grossly unfair. On the waiter's next appearance he voiced his protest. "Wot", he bawled, "Naw chootney for Sambo?"

The question of diet arose again some years later when Middlesex took the field, accompanied by Ted Carris, beside whose majestic girth even Maurice Leyland looked lean and hungry. He was an instant success, and there were many friendly enquiries and speculations as to his habitual fare, the consensus of opinion plumping for rice

87

pudding. On the same occasion there stood in the out-field, in almost painful contrast, an amateur of extreme spareness and angularity. No interest was evinced in his appetite, but a high shouldered, camel-like gait proved very popular, and his frequent excursions round the ring were greeted with great joyful shouts of " Coom on, Lady Godiva ", and exhortations to " throotch oop " his legs.

Bramall Lane has maintained its fame and character without the help of international events. There has been but one Test Match played there, in 1902, when Australia beat England by 143 runs. The collector's piece on that occasion was a pair made by Joe Darling, " c Braund b Barnes ", in both instances. Perhaps, after all, the good partisan Bramall Lanite would rather not have foreigners playing on his sacred soil.

In days gone by, Sheffield was acclaimed as the best in-formed cricket crowd in the world, but the thoughtful amongst them deny that this is true of the present genera-tion. After my recent visit it is a judgement I could endorse.

But if the Championship is in fact the dawn of another glorious era of Yorkshire cricket, t'Lane may again set the standards of first-hand criticism.

CHAPTER TWELVE

The Ideal Cricket Ground

THERE CAN BE FEW, BE HE PLAYER, SPECTATOR or secretary, who has not at one time cast an eye over his favourite cricket ground and speculated how he would have built it had he started from scratch with a free hand and the proceeds of a take-over bid. For the truth is that every historic cricket ground has grown piecemeal from quite humble beginnings; many, now situated in densely populated areas, were peaceful rustic sites when the top-hatted players staged the opening match, with a few benches quite sufficient accommodation for the " gate ".

Everyone is familiar with the early history of Thomas Lord who, pursued by an expanding London, rolled up his precious turf and fitted from Dorset Square to the uncongested peace of Marylebone only to find, in a very few years' time that the builders were once again treading on his outfield. And if it had not been for the foresight and generosity of Mr. William Ward they would have erected their buildings on his next and last halting place. Where, if anywhere, the present ground would have been, had this come about, is hard to guess.

Old Clarke chose an idyllic scene on the banks of the Trent, and caused much umbrage amongst the Nottingham citizens by charging sixpence for admission to his new ground. The Manchester Cricket Club's tenure of their first ground was cut short by the intrusion of an art exhibition upon the scene, but Old Trafford had plenty of nice open fields around so they did not have to move very far.

Once established on a site with some prospect of permanence the newly founded Cricket Club naturally started to build such accommodation as was required, in the first place for members and players, and later for spectators. Unlike New Yorkers who have a passion for tearing down

89

BOWLER'S TURN

"old" buildings of twenty or thirty years' standing, and putting something absolutely modern on the space, in this country we have a great reverence for ancient buildings, and a great reluctance to interfere with them. The cricket world is at least an averagely conservative realm, in addition to which very few clubs have ever been overburdened with cash, so that most of our grounds are the result of solid Victorian building in the first place, with various additions of other periods, and occasional internal rearrangement. Although this is economical, and occasionally picturesque, it can hardly be expected to lead to an ideal situation for all concerned. Recently County Clubs in this country, especially those who cater for Test Matches, have made great efforts, and there has been a very marked improvement in every sphere, but there is no ground I have visited where public, players, press and caterers join in an unqualified unison of praise. Human nature being what it is, this utopian state of affairs is admittedly unlikely, whatever the physical shape of things, but it might be brought a little nearer if the architect could be provided with a free untrammelled space of the required acreage, unlimited funds, and uninterrupted scope for his ideas. It is hard to see these conditions arising in this country, even under the most enlightened Ministry of Sport, but at least one man has had the luxury of seriously planning his ideal cricket ground to the last detail on paper.

Some time ago Mr. W. R. Ainsworth of Stockton-on-Tees wrote to me, apropos of something I had said on the present topic, telling me that he had chosen, as his subject for his architectural degree, a design for a cricket ground. It was planned as a headquarters for the Northumberland County Cricket Club, and Mr. Ainsworth most kindly sent me the full details and some photographs. The designer writes:

Naturally I cannot explain the planning within the clubrooms and restaurants without yourself seeing the drawings, but I will do my best to explain the general layout and conditions.

The siting of the playing square is N.N.W.-S.S.E., the pavilion and clubroom being placed along the line of play. The long room, players' viewing rooms and open viewing terraces for members, players and guests also look along the line of play. You can see from the photographs that the seating sweeps up towards the middle at each end of the ground. This provides for maximum seating directly behind the bowler's arm. Members' seating is directly above the clubroom, and direct access from the stand to the restaurant, bar and lounge is provided.

The clubrooms and pavilion are separated by a kitchen. The kitchen serving members' restaurant and snacks with the clubroom, and players dining within the players' section.

Members are provided with an open court within the clubrooms, where they are able to have coffee or meals in perfect privacy from the general public. It can also be used for a sun lounge.

All facilities are provided within the clubrooms, including indoor nets 150 feet long, squash court, billiards, table tennis, bar, games room and lounge. A special administration section is also included. The rough programme will enable you to see the accommodation provided.

The rectangular block at the west side of the ground is the public restaurant, including a waitress served section and a snack area. Open piazzas and grassed areas around the arena provide for the public to sit and eat sandwiches in comfort, instead of within the stadium itself.

An open promenade runs completely around the ground at 12 ft.-6 in. level and provides for easy circulation of public to any part of the ground, without disturbing spectators.

The break in the top tier of seating at the east and west side enable everybody within the ground, wherever they sit, and indeed players themselves, to look out into the treed areas. A feeling of freedom and open being produced rather than complete enclosure.

The space beneath the promenade is utilised for public toilets, licensed bars, snack bars, and storage space.

A special system of sight screen is devised. A canvas blind painted white can be pulled down between every main structure. So wherever the pitch occurs the canvas blind directly behind it will be pulled down. The others will remain open.

The heating system is electric thermal storage. Heat being transmitted by heating panels within the ceiling. A quick and efficient heat is produced.

Mr. Ainsworth seems to have thought of everything.

Despite a certain strain of architectural blood in my veins I am wholly unqualified to pronounce on the merits of the general design. I can but say that the general effect is, to me, quite splendid, and I would be delighted to be bidden as player, pressman or spectator. Perhaps, with cricket spreading rapidly all over the world and fresh populations springing up in new places, I shall one day be able to descend from the press box to the sunken piazza in search of a cooling draught and fresh inspiration, on some foreign field.

CHAPTER THIRTEEN

People in Glasshouses

MR. DUMBLE PUT DOWN THE WATERING can and surveyed the row of wallflowers which surrounded the pavilion rails.

"Cooming on very nice," he said, nodding approvingly at his handiwork. "Nothin' to satisfy a man like givin' a helping hand to the wunders o' nature".

With this profound reflection Mr. Dumble seated himself heavily on the front bench and, puffing his pipe into renewed activity, addressed himself to the small group of horticultural advisers about him:

"I've 'eard soom folk talk of Kent as t'garden of England, he said, but if you was to ask me it doesn't compare with Loamshire. Specially district round Lumperton, not twenty mile from 'ere, they grow fruit an' flowers an' veg't-ables such as you'll find in no other place in England, nor any other country, coom to that. Whole place is that beautiful it might ha' been painted by yon police constable chap, wot with trees and grass and all.

When I were int' side we used to play wot you might call country house match ont' village ground to raise funds for Canon Driver's charities. And though small it were a reet loovely ground wot had been presented to village by woon o' General Picklethwaite-Spelby's ancestors, and it were divided from his land by briar hedge. And ont' other side o' ground lived Admiral ffuttock-Shroud, a very fierce retired sea dog.

It so happened that squire at this time, General Sir Witherington Picklethwaite-Spelby and Admiral ffuttock-Shroud were deadly rivals in a'most everything, but specially in gardening. They both thought that with a couple o' hours a week they could ha' improved t' Garden of Eden out of all recognition, and to 'ear 'em talk you'd ha' thought that Lumperton was oasis saved from desert by their efforts alone. And neither would allow that t'other knew anything. General calls Admiral an ignorant labourer, and Admiral talks about General as a cloombsy sapper, so that annual Flower Show is an agony to whole neighbourhood. After a few years they can't get any joodges in Loamshire, so they have to send for Lundon chaps—but they never coom more than wunce.

Well one year lawyer chap named Quillbeck, wots made a bit o' mooney, goes to live int' district and takes oop gardening very serious too. When t'other two hear hes going to enter for Flower Show they laff, and General says it'll be nice for that worm groubbing ffuttock-Shroud to have a bit of coompany at bottom of list. But at same time they're both uneasy cos they know this Quillbeck is as crafty as they coom.

Poomkins is their thing, and it seems that this year fashionable line is t'Patagonia Princess or soochlike, and if anywoon talks o' growing anything else poomkin' men joost smile superior. Special prize is offered for them as they're very delicate and hard to grow and nobody knows much about 'em but General and Admiral make a great stoody of 'em, and soon they're in their green'ouses watching each oother like cat and dog. General's had his green'ous moved down nearer to hedge to get more sun; so he can see Admiral training his telescope on 'im from his, which is back a bit from wall on t'oother side of ground. Meantime Quillbeck is working away very secret.

When we go to play match feeling is rooning very 'igh in Lumperton, and chap named Alfie Hustleton has made book on' result of contest. He finds it very hard to get reliable information, but General's favourite at evens with Admiral at six to four, and Quillbeck well down betting at one hundred to eight. For time being however excitement has turned to match, and General and Admiral relax sufficient to bow to each oother very stiff when they meet int' morning.

It's a loovely day and, as usual, Lumperton and District are captained by t'Admiral who says they'll bat first so a crowd will get a bit o' foon int' afternoon. Theers always lots of folks as they coom in from all round, and soom of 'em from Spliceshire collieries are inclined to be a bit roof, and very keen to get their bob's worth.

Well we keeps 'em battin' till lunchtime and sees that t'Admiral gets a nice few roons, so as he'll be in good form at table. Loonch is under trees and theers pies, and hams, an' beef an' mooton, an' beer an' cider, and after that theers port wine, but meself I has anoother pint. But Admiral likes a glass o' port and he's had quite woon or two when it's time to play again.

He's just got back to pavilion, wot he calls "Ward Room," when oop cooms Quillbeck bowing and smirking. "How are you, sir?" he says "Wot a beautiful scene, to be sure".

"Is it not, Quillbeck" say Admiral, very 'earty "This coontry life will make a man out of even a land lubber like you".

And Quillbeck sniggers and rubs his 'ands together.

"I've just been admiring t'Generals new green'ouse" he says "I trust it is not dangerously exposed t' enemy's fire"!

Admiral scowls at green'ouse which is about square leg, and not fifteen yards over boundary.

"It 'ud serve him right if soomwoon put ball through t'damn thing" he says "Save 'im humiliation at show, too".

"Ho ho" says Quillbeck "That would divert the hoi poloi no end. I've got a good mind to offer every man who strikes it a shilling a time".

"I'll make that a guinea" says Admiral.

"Good Gracious me" says Quillbeck "D'you hear that"? he says to George Damson who's passing by "Theer's a guinea for every man who hits ball int' green-house. He he".

95

BOWLER'S TURN

"That'll cost you a bit" says George, and he rooshes int' dressing room to pass word to his cronies.

Theer's great stir amoong our batters when they hear this and, wot with Admiral opening bowling from t'far end, they reckon its worth a coople o' county matches all round. Sure enoof first over George Damson hits a ballooner that drops through roof, and second over he hits a skimmer that goes in woon side and out t'other, afore it bounces off tree and cooms back in again. He's scratchin' notches ont' back of bat when soodenly theer's a tremendous scene. General has coom down garden to watch cricket, and seen damage to glass. When Admiral bowls another full toss which is hit just over green'ouse he sees wots afoot right away.

He tries to roosh ont' field, but his guests catch him in time and beg 'im to restrain his language; but he shakes 'em off and roons back oop garden. He cooms back with head gardener and several assistants in time to see ball take big pane out of t'door. He's still very athletic at sixty-seven and he seizes ball and throws it fifty yards away over trees. He seems quite oopset, and we sees that gardeners have all got fish nets. He lines 'em oop and stands in froont with his arms folded and his face bright purple.

At that moment Mr. Quillbeck cooms to me and he says "Doomble" he says "This is terrible. You're a safe field. Coom with me and see if we can help t'General".

So I goes round with 'im and we arrives joost as ball cooms whizzin' over again. 'Ead gardener goes to net it and General roons to catch it with resoolt that gardener nets t'General and ball takes him bang ont' froont stood, and between t'three of 'em they take anoother coople of panes. When we disentangle 'im General stands gnashing his teeth, but says nowt cos he sees that wot he's got to say is beyond woon alf strangled man.

Crowd on our side of t'ground are enjoying themselves very mooch, but crowd ont' far side are getting very impatient. Presently soom chaps start barracking, and saying they payed their bobs to see proper cricket not a roody farce.

"This is most oontoward, my dear General" says Quillbeck. "Indeed" he says "I fear that t'roofer element int' crowd might be incited to riot at any moment".

General looks at 'im as he might at staff officer who says that t'enemy's at gates, and we sees that it's not for nowt that he's got four rows o' medals. He draws himself oop very stiff and says to me:

"Doomble" he says "Be good enoof to organise this 'ere party in defence of my property. Time has coom to launch counter attack".

He turns very sharp and goes behind green'ouse, and next we sees him walkin' round ground with garden hose sloong over his shoulder. Admiral's still bowling away and every time ball is hit towards green'ouse he laffs fit to boost. But crowd ont' far side are very awkward by now and theer's soom commotion. Several chaps are standin' oop now and shouting that they want proper cricket.

Then soodenly we hear General's voice behind them.

"Sit down theer and behave yourselves" he shouts.

"Sit down yerself and shoot oop" shouts big bulky-chap, wot looks like ring leader. "We want our bobs worth".

"Very good, sir" says General "Here it is".

And he oops with hose which he's screwed into tap and starts to spray crowd, specially big chap wots meantime turned back to game.

At first chaps are very poozled by sooden change int' weather but, as they turns for shelter, they sees 'ose and a fearsome howl goes oop. As woon man they head for General shouting that they'll lynch 'im; but he stands his ground and, water pressure in Lumperton being very 'igh, squirts cap clean off big chap's 'ead. Then he drops 'ose and nips through gate, and starts roonin' towards Admiral's green'ouse through trees with crowd after 'im.

Meantime game's stopped and Admiral seein' he's oondoon rooshes to boundary hollerin' for his 'ead gardener.

"All hands to stations!" he shouts "Bottleman, stand by to repel boarders".

But he's too late, and General dodges past Bottleman and his mates and gets int' green'ouse. As gardeners go down before crowd he cooms out again with armful o' tomatoes, and lets go a volley afore he pulls door to and locks himself in. Theer's anoother roar of anger as crowd surge forward, and has door down with a crash of broken glass. General lets leaders have a coople more tomatoes and then nips through door at the far end. Next moment crowd have reached that and it flies open outwards, soomthing builder had never intended.

Joost at that moment posse of police, wots been mustered very 'asty when crowd have looked oogly, coom oop behind General, and crowd int' green'ouse change their mind. Fine body o' men Loamshire Police and, as only woon chap can get through door at a time, most of 'em make their own emergency exits, as you might say, and next moment place looks like it had been strook by bomb. Crowd disperse very rapid, havin' dispersed quite a bit of Admiral's garden int' process, and police have all their time took oop trying to keep Admiral from gettin' 'old of General.

But by time they've been escorted back to pavilion they've both cooled down a lot, and they fair quail oonder eye of Canon Driver, wot was joost settin' out with collection box, when row started. When he bids 'em very stern to step into Secretary's office with 'im they looks like coople of schoolboys going to 'eadmaster's stoody.

I happened to be near door, and can hear 'im addressing 'em very powerful ont' proper behaviour of responsible citizens and Christian gentlemen. When they coom out they're very chastened and Admiral says,

"General" he says "I feel that I am the chief offender in this most melancholy affair. I beg you to join me in a glass of wine".

And General says he'll be mooch honoured, and he hopes that all between them is now forgot. Game is resumed, and Admiral puts anoother bowler on so crowd settle down, and everywoon has a very nice time.

Well it so 'appens that weather for next fortnight is finest anywoon can remember and wot with news of t'battle spreadin' round fine big crowd turns oop for Lumperton Show. I goes over as I thinks it might be very interesting. Alfie Hustleton says that General and Admiral have gone right out int' bettin', and Quillbeck is now favourite and has backed himself pretty heavy.

It's a nice pleasant day and at last theer's big moment for t'joodging o' poomkins. They've got very learned professor chap from Lundon, wot knows more about poomkins than any livin man; and theer's breathless 'oosh as he starts round. He scratches his chin 'ooms and 'aws at Quillbeck's lot, and examines next two or three very careful; then he gets to General's and Admiral's wot are at end o' line. When he sees 'em his eyes light oop.

"My, me" he says "Wot loovely poomkins"!

Then he examines them close and compares woon with t'ooter. After a long time he turns to coompany.

"These 'ere" he says "Are that superior to all t'oothers that I feel it only fair that they should jointly share t'first prize".

Theer's a great burst of applause at this and then Professor says

"Ladies and Gentlemen" he says "Now for a few words ont' science of poomkin growin'. Soon poomkins" he says "are swashbookling warriors equal to all nature's weapons. Soon are hard headed businessmen able to cope with all circumstances, and soon are sinewy athletes. But not so t'Patagonian Princess. She is a delicate fragile creature of royal birth, demanding that her every whim shall be cossetted and indoolged. Give her your loove gentlemen" says Professor with great emotion "and she will smile back at you with all her intoxicatin' beauty. But make to 'er woon off 'and gesture and she will pine". "Now you, sir " says Professor to Quillbeck, wots standing theer very glum, "You have oonwittingly illreated

99

BOWLER'S TURN

Princess. In warm weather like this she cries for t'clean fresh breezes of 'er native land, her loovely body calls out for t'breath you 'ave denied her. She has lain theer sad and stifled while, if only for a coople o' days, you had opened windows t'floosh o' beauty would have flooded to 'er cheek. And so, ladies and gentlemen" says Professor "Remember the message I leave with you today.

" T'key to t'Princess's 'eart is bound oop in woon word— *ventilation*".

CHAPTER FOURTEEN

Tweak House

THERE IS ONE SCORE UPON WHICH I will defend the batsman. It is that he is quite frequently blamed for dull and dreary play when it is really the fault of the bowler.

There are in fact more dull bowlers than dull batsmen. They run an inordinately long way to deliver the ball at an inconvenient pace to an inaccessible place with unerring accuracy. They count their success in terms of maiden overs, frustration and exasperation. And their evil influence extends beyond the scope of their actual operations, for now, if more than four are gathered together on the on-side, the ball has but to pass outside the batsman's legs for him to switch his skirts away and assume an air of persecution. The whole muddled scene is then resolved by the addlepate in the outer who deafeningly directs the bowler, to "Baowl at the shockin' wicket".

But these, as Holmes was heard to remark, are deep waters. Let us rejoice that there are still some very interesting bowlers. Their influence on the game was strikingly illustrated for us camp-followers in Australia as we travelled round with Peter May's team. There was quite a lot of interesting play in the early stages but the best entertainment was the match against New South Wales who boasted three leg spinners, a bonny sight for eyes starved of this type of bowling. May made the best hundred of the tour against them and for this he justly received full recognition but I doubt if the bowlers got much credit for their share of the entertainment. It was because they were such an interesting lot that May was enabled to exercise his full artistry.

They were led by Australia's new fast bowler, Rorke, a blonde giant whose majestic approach to the crease is something between a buffalo charging and Siegfried's journey to the Rhine. On arrival he is liable to skid several feet past it and, in moments of excitement, his action is more enthusiastic than orthodox. His pace is tremendous and his variation of direction so generous and unpredictable that assistants as far afield as gully and short leg, who normally look at the bat, are well advised to keep a sharp eye in his direction, with a view to taking instant evasive action. His wicket-keeper gets the same amount and type of exercise as a tumbler on one of these spring mattresses. Nary a dull moment here. Above all there were three legbreakers, Benaud, Philpott and O'Neill, to keep the proceedings alive throughout the day. Typically, Philpott, a big spinner of the ball, beat May decisively for a start, and in the same over was smacked for three whistling fours for his pains. Whatever his faults the true tweaker is never repressive or boring. In truth, the greater his faults the less so he is likely to be.

I am not concerned with the impeccable Barnes or O'Reilly, who turned the ball from the leg, but with the devotee who curls his wrist up in the region of his flask pocket and, with bared teeth and countenance distorted with effort, gives it all he's got. What matter if it doesn't land quite in the right place, so long as it bursts like a bomb in a beehive; this is art for art's sake——even if some captains do not appreciate the point. If this ball is belted far into the most expensive seats the occupants at least have had their money's worth. If the next one drops in the right place to puncture an inflated batsman, thrashing furiously in the wrong direction, they have had a handsome bonus. That is the true tweaker, the optimist, the sanguine gambler; the serpent among bowlers, venomous but vulnerable.

The bias from the leg was, of course, the original and natural one in underhand days, but its application by the overarm bowler called for a complicated and rather unnatural technique. That grand old Middlesexian, Billy Williams, used to say that he had invented this while bowling to an early Australian team in the nets. But even as a fellow clubman I am unable to support this claim in the light of history, and it is more likely, that the modern leg-break evolved from a technique similar to that of W.G.'s round-arm top spinners. It was pioneered in international cricket by A. G. Steel.

The greatest innovation in the era of overarm bowling came with Bosanquet's invention or discovery of the googly. The impact of this on the uninitiated must have been akin to that of Lamborn's newly-invented underhand off-break on the All-England Eleven on Broadhalfpenny. "This new trick of his so bothered the Kent and Surrey men that they tumbled out one after another as though they had been picked off by a rifle corps". To the decently brought up batsman the first off-breaking leg-break must have smacked of the the Indian rope trick.

It would seem that the inventor was not among the greatest practical exponents, but succeeded chiefly on grounds of novelty. It was the South African school, Vogler, White, Faulkner and Snooke, who brought the leg-break - cum - googly to its highest pitch of perfection. Schwartz was another sort of phenomenon in that he could only bowl the googly, and the more he strove to master the leg-break the more he turned from the off.

Faulkner was my first employer, and a rare good bowler when I first knew him in his late forties. He spun abundantly, disguised the wrong 'un from all but the hawk-eyed, and was remarkably accurate. But he himself said that Vogler was the best of the breed, over medium in pace, with a knife-like wrong 'un. In fact Faulkner ranked him in his best moments next only to the great Sydney Barnes. Slightly later came Pegler, the last of the great South Africans.

Their mantle blew across the Indian Ocean to alight on the shoulders of an Australian dentist named Hordern, who, in a losing series against England, took thirty-two wickets for twenty-four apiece with slow flighted spinners, which he delivered from a longish run. He was succeeded by Mailey, who spun the ball more than anyone could remember having seen it spun before, and revelled in its every rotation. Even on the grey steel Australian wickets of his era he would achieve a certain bias quite early in the match. Percy Fender has said that in playing him it was advisable to aim at the fielder as the turn of the ball would always carry it to one or other side. My only personal experience of batting against Arthur was on a village wicket in Sussex a couple of years ago, a surface on which he produced results worthy of the fifth of November. I did, however, bowl with him. He recalls in his book a Sunday during a Test Match when he and I spent an enthralling hour, bowling a ball to and fro on a stately Lancastrian lawn. Reprimanded by a cagey manager for blowing state secrets, Mailey replied that this was art, and as such international!

His successor, Clarrie Grimmett, was maybe the greatest slow leg breaker of all time on his form in this country. His wrong 'un was a moderate ball, easy to spot and not particularly vicious, but his command of the leg-break was consummate, and his quick in-dipping top spinner a deadly weapon. Morover he *knew* how to bowl, and bestowed on each customer the lavish individual care and attention of a Harley Street specialist. He was at Adelaide for the last Test Match played there, nearing seventy, seemingly unchanged, the same neat spare twinkling figure. He still bowls in his garden but complains that he has lost a bit of nip off the wicket.

Grimmett's latter day partner, Bill O'Reilly, was the best bowler of his type (if indeed he had a type), I have ever seen, a combination of spin, flight, bounce and mathematical accuracy. The leg-break and top spinner he rolled at anything up to medium pace. The googly he spun sharply without warning from the hand but, so the experts said, it was detectable in the air by a difference of flight. He was a splendidly hostile performer and, while one had the impression that Grimmett liked batsmen as a cat likes a mouse, it was apparent that O'Reilly regarded them as a mongoose does a snake.

Although the googly was invented in England the cult

has never flourished so strongly in this country as in Australia. Long ago D. W. Carr emerged as an England bowler at the venerable age of thirty-seven and "young" Jack Hearne augmented his superb leg-breaks with an occasional "boosie" of fair quality until he sadly broke his wrist.

Between the wars "Tich" Freeman was easily the most consistent of the googly bowlers but lack of success in Australia and South Africa prejudiced his chances of playing against Australia in this country, perhaps unfairly; Walter Robins was in 1929 and 1930 the very best of his type with pace, real spin and a particularly well disguised wrong 'un. Douglas Wright had his great times, but in recent years wet summers and ill-made pitches have made off-spinners a better proposition in this country. A spell of good summers or the better faster wickets resulting from covering may well revive the art; but it will take time. Let us hope not too long, for in its absence the game is that much duller.

CHAPTER FIFTEEN

A Sailor's Tale

WHEN WRITING THIS BOOK I WAS, IN common with a great many other people, saddened to hear of the death of an old Middlesex colleague. Richard Hill was a very good all-round athlete and, in addition to being a fine fluent batsman around number five, he was a most popular member of the side being, as they say, something of a character. He was a very lovable man, and although disposed to be shy and modest, had much humour and a great enjoyment of life. He also had a positive flair for attracting improbable, if harmless, adventure.

For instance, it could only have happened to Richard that, when in the deep at Oxford, a lady dog took refuge between his legs so that, for a fearsome ten minutes, he stood like a beleaguered lighthouse in the midst of a vast swirling, snarling canine sea. To him alone the agony of risking his all (and more) on the ranker outsider in a field of three in a desperate "get out", only to see his beast straddled on the last jump, its legs frantically thrashing the air, as a remounted favourite thundered round the course in hot pursuit. (Don't worry, it won—but just.)

Many other adventures of a similarly unlikely nature befell him in our cricketing days, so you see what I mean.

Not so long ago I ran into him at a squash match and, perhaps it was because we celebrated our meeting in pink gin, that I was reminded of Richard's career in war-time, which started at a ripe age when he joined up, and became Ordinary Seaman Hill. I was first aware of this addition to our main line of defence when I saw him at Lord's, resplendent in bell-bottom trousers, berating an old school chum, who happened to be dressed as a Major General. Recalling this as we drank, and knowing his propensity for adventure, it struck me his nautical experiences might be worth hearing; so I asked him if anything untoward had befallen him during that time.

"Well", said Richard after some reflection, "one thing happened which I thought was rather funny."

When I heard it I thought it was rather funny too, not to say remarkable, so here it is, although I may have got some of the maritime terms a bit askew.

It appears that Richard's career, if hardly Nelsonian, progressed satisfactorily, so that eventually he was commissioned and posted to an escort vessel. This gallant ship, which we may call H.M.S. Bumbleduck so as not to offend any of her company, was commanded by a war-time sailor, a man of strong individual mind whose original ideas of sailing a ship sometimes, in fact frequently—well practically always failed to coincide with the accepted precepts of higher authority. This meant that, always including the accepted enemy, he was usually engaged in hostilities on at least two fronts; but as this suited his temperament, he was not inclined to yield nor alter his ways. Thus when they found themselves one December at the tail end of an Atlantic convoy, a very exacting rôle, it was not long before they attracted the attention of the Senior Officer Escort.

This man was also of strong character, with a mastery of invective which strained the signal book to bursting point. Richard informed me that the best efforts of a U-boat and Luftwaffe were but pin-pricks compared with the verbal barrage which hourly smote H.M.S. Bumbleduck with hurricane force. It seemed they could do no right, but eventually the ordeal ended, and they arrived at the mouth of the Irish river for which the convoy was destined, and the Senior Officer delivered them a farewell message.

He took quite a bit of trouble over the wording of it, but it was roughly to the effect that if he ever made contact with H.M.S. Bumbleduck again, he hoped it would be at the extreme range of his depth sounding apparatus.

BOWLER'S TURN

Furthermore he considered their state of training to be such that he had arranged a little practice for them, so they would take the convoy just leaving across to the Clyde. This was rather a blow as it would probably mean missing the only leave train, and so Christmas at home. However, "theirs not to reason why", and off they went, to return two days later. This was smart time and they were still just starters for the leave train.

But where the Senior Officer had left off, nature had taken on, and their last hopes of the train were damped by a thick fog which overhung the estuary. However, they crept cautiously forward, and soon picked up their Irish pilot who had been patiently awaiting them. It was immediately apparent that he had not devoted his enforced leisure to the furtherance of the temperance movement, and his first instructions almost led to disaster. There was a nasty grinding, bumping noise from the bottom of the ship, and she checked and then shot forward again. The Captain cried out in pain for his Asdic, but the pilot made light of that, pointing out that the "machaine" would be wanting repairing anyway. He was enlarging on this theme when a shout from the helmsman drew his attention to a buoy dead ahead. He peered at this with professional interest.

"Oi'm wonderin' phwat buoy that moight be ", he mused, " and which soide we should be takin'."

To avoid running it down the helmsman uttered a silent prayer and went hard-a-port.

"Och well ", said the pilot, " and ye've missed the damn thing anyway."

Further up the river all had gone well. The convoy was snugly berthed, various duties efficiently completed and the leave party was aboard the train which was just starting down the single line, which was the only exit from the port. The S.O.E. read his mail contentedly and thought of home and family, as the train chugged slowly on its way. The line wound along the river bank where the fog lay thick, so the driver and his mate strained their eyes for the signal lights. At length, rounding a bend the driver espied the welcome green light and opened the regulator full. All was well and the engine bounded forward on her happy mission.

But no! You see, it wasn't a signal, but H.M.S. Bumbleduck's starboard light, and a sudden break in the mist revealed her in her entirety, bravely breasting the waters. Nor was it the ethereal beauty of the scene which so electrified the driver and his mate, but rather the fact that she was headed straight for the bank. As they looked she bravely breasted the fore-shore, her bows snipped the railway line neatly in two and, pushing inland another few yards, she settled slap across the metals with a contented sigh. The driver and his mate stood on everything and then jumped for it.

The little tank engine came to a shuddering standstill under the bridge thirty feet above, and stood hissing with indignation. Doors flew open the whole length of the train, out poured the passengers, and great was their astonishment to see their old consort bang across the only road to home and happiness.

There was a slight pause before another door opened and the S.O.E. stepped out, a fine brisk, commanding figure. As he advanced the company respectfully made way for him; but it seemed that as he advanced his step grew heavier, and the fierceness of his presence fell from him like a discarded duffle-coat.

He surveyed the land-locked Bumbleduck, the shattered line, and eventually his eye bent upwards to the embarrassed trio on the bridge far above.

When he spoke it was without rancour, almost in tones of admiration.

"All right", he said, "you win."

CHAPTER SIXTEEN

The Kelpie

YOU PROBABLY DIDN'T KNOW THAT I once unintentionally was instrumental in winning a Test Match for Australia.

It is a story which goes back to the spacious days of the 'thirties, to be exact, 1934, when I was playing an August week's cricket in Scotland. The base of operations was an old baronial home, and the opposition supplied by the surrounding clubs. The entertainment was liberally supplied by the surrounding gentry and glamour in the shape of dinners, dances and parties.

For various reasons I had played but little first class cricket that season so that it was with surprise, not to say astonishment, that one morning during the week I read, over a mound of kedgeree, a wire saying, "Are you available to play against Australia Oval Aug. . . .", signed "Perrin, Chairman, Selectors." Astonishment soon gave way to scepticism. I could visualise a number of old friends hearing of a modest success at Brechin seizing the opportunity of two bobs-worth of fun (the reply was prepaid). Caution was the thing. Not to be the sucker of all time was one thing, but to be the first cricketer in history to ignore a selection committee summons was something too. I made no comment and stuffed the form into my pocket.

Another pleasant day's play went by and in the evening we went to another ball—I'm not certain it wasn't, like the one celebrated in song, at Kirriemuir. It was on leaving this sparkling function in the small hours that I should have realised I was enmeshed in a train of events beyond my control. On the way out I collided with a Kelpie—Scots for gremlin, but, being Celtic, the craftiest and most venomous type and this one took an instant fancy to me. I was first aware of this attachment when our car blew up two miles from home, and the usually discreet butler opened the door as dawn broke, cursing into the beard our new pal was playfully tweaking.

If I had any doubts about the source of the telegram the morning's papers dispelled them. I was news. The press, always kind to me, were justifiably aggrieved. The leading National Dailies gave it the front page, publishing my picture in one corner and that of Bill Voce, also a photogenic man, in the other. "Why Peebles, why not Voce", they said. It was a point, and I digested it with mixed feelings. But old Kelpie was right at my elbow.

"Go on", he said, "Not yellow, are you?"

I pulled out the prepaid form, addressed it to "Perrin, Lord's", and wrote "Delighted. Will be there if not lynched on the road."

We took the local field a bit later that morning in an indifferent state of training. I started the day with a full-toss, and the ball was slung back to the middle by a muscular boy in the crowd. As I went to collect it the Kelpie put his hand over my eyes. To humans, a Kelpie's hand looks like a lot of black spots so naturally my focus was disturbed. I just got a touch on the ball which knocked the top joint of my spinning finger back at a neat right angle. However, help was immediately forthcoming from Arthur Hazlerigg, an opponent of Varsity days, who seized my finger in a deft powerful grip and, nipping the joint back again, pronounced it as good as new. By lunch time it looked as though I was sucking an over-ripe banana and on returning to London it was X-rayed and found to be broken into the bargain.

I notified the authorities of this disaster, but turned up at the Oval on the appointed day as I would at least have a good seat, and the catering was of a high order. My Kelpie pal came along but, tiring of me as a broken reed, took an instant liking to Bob Wyatt, captain of England, who was already in a bit of trouble. The selectors had given him a battery of fast bowlers, but no regular slips and no outfielders. Hedley Verity was the only slow bowler, and it did not look much like his wicket. Pat Hendren was crocked and, when Frank Woolley, at the age of forty-seven, was hauled in, that peerless judge, Sir Pelham Warner, prophesied that being unfamiliar with O'Reilly he would straightway be caught at short leg. He was.

Anyway, such were Bob's misgivings about navigating this unwieldy ship that, despite the wodge of splints and bandage on my finger, he insisted that I should play. It took quite some time to convince him of the impossibility of this, at the end of which all three went out to toss—Bob, Bill Woodfull and the Kelpie. Naturally Bob lost.

Australia started off on a perfect Oval wicket. "Nobby" Clark went on first change and at twenty-one hit Bill Brown's off-stump with a real beauty. Enter Donald George Bradman. His first five scoring strokes were all fours which seemed to whet his appetite as, with Bill Ponsford going nicely, the next wicket fell at 472. England had a sad day in the field, and Bob twice missed Ponsford off chances he would normally have swallowed. He thought he had lost the ball against the banks of spectators, but of course, I know better. Naturally next day was also disastrous for the home team. England had lost five wickets for 142 in reply to Australia's 701 when Leyland and Ames started to play magnificently. They had added eighty-five when Ames strained his back. Only nine wickets fell as Bill Bowes was carted off to hospital to be operated upon for a common but painful complaint. When England took the field again Woolley kept wicket in the absence of Ames, but the out-fielding was greatly strengthened by the two Surrey substitutes, Gregory and McMurray.

Next morning Bowes bravely returned to the stricken field and bowled magnificently but, when all was said and done, England had 708 to make on the last innings. Walters went for one and poor Frank Woolley, going to drive McCabe before he was off the mark, holed out at mid-off. As he turned dejectedly for home I was standing with Capt. Wyatt who made an historic remark.

"Never mind", he sighed. "He kept wicket very well." At that he sat heavily on the nearest chair which, entering into the spirit of the thing, collapsed underneath him. England's batting did likewise so the Aussies (with one given but invisible man) won by 562 runs. As they did so I felt rather than heard the skirl of insane laughter.

One last point. I turned to Wisden, one of a set recently acquired from a distinguished cricket writer, to check my facts and figures. Apparently this match had also attracted the previous owner's attention as the place was marked by a faded leaf from a tear-off calendar. The "Thought for today" seemed to me to sum up the whole thing. It read, "Hurray! Blister my kidneys, 'tis a frost! The dahlias are dead."

To which, speaking as a student of the occult, I would add "not 'arf".

Last Overs

Modern Times
Timely Arrival
Educating the Young
The Hand of the Bowler
Scoreboard

CHAPTER SEVENTEEN

Modern Times

THE CHANGES IN THE ACTUAL GAME of cricket as between pre- and post-war eras are really remarkably small when they are considered against the vast changes of the world in which it is played. But changes there are and they can be traced directly to the alterations in general circumstances.

Cricket, except for the comparatively few top-ranking players, is relatively less well paid than in pre-war days, when a county professional's earnings were generally greater than the industrial worker's. Thus counties could attract promising young players whose modern counterparts are more reluctant to risk a secure job for the hazards of professional cricket, whatever its glamour and attractions. Amateurs who are not in some way dependent on the game for their livelihood are so rare as to be almost non-existent. Paradoxically the standards of amateur cricket in the last decade have been exceedingly high, and this is attributable to the fact that, unless an amateur is of sufficient calibre, it is hardly worth while his struggling to keep going. Only the outstanding can expect to be offered jobs, such as county secretaryships or salesmen, which will enable them to devote sufficient time to play regularly. The man such as the Rev. David Sheppard, whose job is completely unconnected with cricket, has a few seasons' glory and then, turning to his profession or vocation, is seen on a few rare occasions.

For those who do reach the top, cricket can be very lucrative. The modern players' opportunities are efficiently exploited by professional managers or agents, popularly known as "ten per centers", who are thoroughly familiar with the market in advertising, journalism and salesmanship. Many may regard this exploitation as slightly sordid, even objectionable, but anyone who has had dealings with professional sport realises that a performer has a limited span and that, when it is over, he is very rapidly forgotten. In cricket alone there have been, over the years, altogether too many tragic cases of those who have enjoyed fame and reasonable fortune and dissipated them without regard for the years of oblivion to come. It is surely better that the individual should make proper provision for himself and his family, even if people, not faced with such problems, are occasionally censorious. However, I am not for this moment concerned with the rights or wrongs of the situation but its effect on the era and its play.

There is a greater degree of publicity given to cricket than ever before. It is, also, through the medium of television, more intimate and personal in its nature than in pre-war days. Every sporting star is now a familiar figure to his every admirer or critic. His appearance, voice, tastes, views and personality are from time to time closely studied in a million homes. He is thus splendid journalistic copy, and any achievement or indiscretion has a personal impact, whereas his predecessor was normally but a name and a newspaper photograph.

These and other factors have changed the collective and individual attitude of players towards the game, especially in the higher realms. Thus, as I said when looking forward from an earlier age, there is liable to be a natural reluctance on the part of a prudent captain or player to take risks.

Curiously enough the brightest period of English cricket in terms of play was in the first few years of the resumption, when the country was living in the utmost austerity. The joy of playing cricket again was sufficient to outweigh many shortcomings, and England's rather dismal showing against the other major powers was patiently borne in anticipation of better things to come. The first real campaign was led by Hammond, the lone remaining great figure of his generation of batsmen. His expedition to Australia in 1946-47 was recognised as being premature from a tactical point of view, but wholly desirable by wider considerations. It was at least as successful as could have been hoped but it brought the captain little satisfaction, and he retired from the scene.

This was in sad contrast to Bradman who, after a few preliminary moments of uncertainty, returned to bestride England with his seven-league boots. They were, in fact, fifty-five-over boots for this was the allotted span of the new ball upon which he based his destructive power. When it had lost its shine Toshack kept the batsmen in check until Miller and Lindwall could spring into action again.

This was a severe strain on the English batting. Hutton, Washbrook, Compton, Edrich and Yardley had their great moments, but English batsmanship was otherwise at a low ebb. Bedser stood alone in a bowling side hard pressed by a titanic batting order.

But the cricket was most interesting. This tremendous batting order scored at a good pace, even if Bradman was only a reminder of the destructive force he once was. Barnes, Morris, Miller, Hassett were all attractive stroke players. Lindwall was the most interesting of fast bowlers and, with Miller and Johnston, made a perfect trio of seamers. The only element lacking from the spectator's point of view in this otherwise well armed team was a first class spin section, and in this department England were better served than their victorious visitors.

Several good summers helped to make it a happy if not particularly distinguished period of English cricket, and Compton and Edrich gave the most interesting entertainment on the good pitches available. There was, notwithstanding, a good deal of depression when the West Indies won a series in this country although, looking back, it does not seem to be such a disgrace to lose to a side which boasted the three W's, and Ramadhin and Valentine, all in top form. Freddy Brown did most gallantly in Australia but, although he astonished everyone with his own achievements, we only won a single Test Match. It was not until

England was led by a professional captain that any material gain was made.

Hutton's succession to the captaincy was given a mixed reception. His opponents based their objections on different grounds. To many, deeply imbued with tradition, the appointment of a professional captain was wrong in principle and, in their view, would automatically give rise to certain difficulties. Others were perfectly ready to accept a professional captain and recognised that it was a matter in accord with the progressive and democratic spirit of the age, but had doubts about Hutton's personal qualifications. These doubts, founded largely upon his reserve and caution, were shared by a variety of players, amateur and professional, and also by sections of the press and public. On the other side there was, especially amongst the public, a tremendous support for Hutton as England's leader; and amongst many more intimately connected with the game a strong feeling that, if not the ideal choice in every respect, he was the only possible man for the job.

Once appointed, Hutton guided his side through a home series with India, rested for the winter and then set about the major operation of a home series against Australia. This he won by a narrow margin, but his side had some alarming passages. He showed himself to be a painstaking rather than inspired tactician, but apart from a bad error of judgement at Leeds when Australia got ahead of the clock, made no real blunder.

The real test of his capacity for captaincy in the widest sense came with his tour of the West Indies. I was not present and so cannot express a first-hand opinion, but the tour was manifestly no more than a qualified success. The incidents which occurred and the behaviour of individuals on either side were hard to see in proper perspective, so emphatic were the views expressed by the contending parties, but the overall impression was that the controlling hand was not sufficiently decisive, nor the diplomacy equal to a complicated and delicate situation. For this the captain could not be held fully responsible,

High Priest. Wilfred Rhodes ponders the situation.

The wooden walls of old England. Herbert Sutcliffe.

Character and courage. Maurice Leyland.

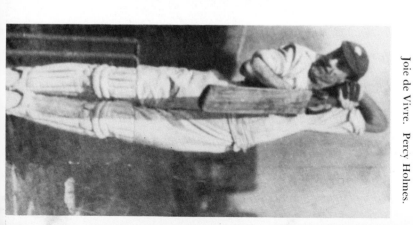

Joie de Vivre. Percy Holmes.

Line and rhythm. Harold Larwood.

The Master.

Virtuoso. George Gunn.

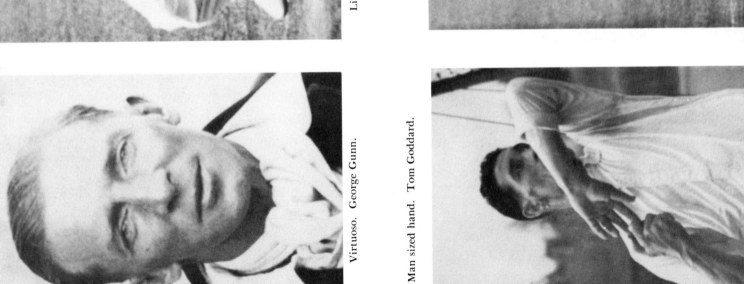

Man sized hand. Tom Goddard.

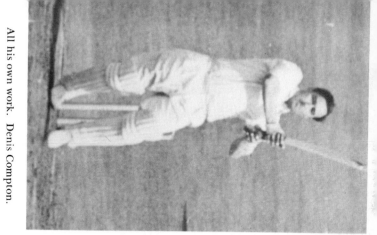

All his own work. Denis Compton.

The old firm. Hutton and Washbrook.

Not in the text book either. W. J. Edrich.

Easy does it through the gap.
Colin Cowdrey.

How to enjoy the bouncer. Norman O'Neill.

After the bottle party. Workers try to separate glass from grass.

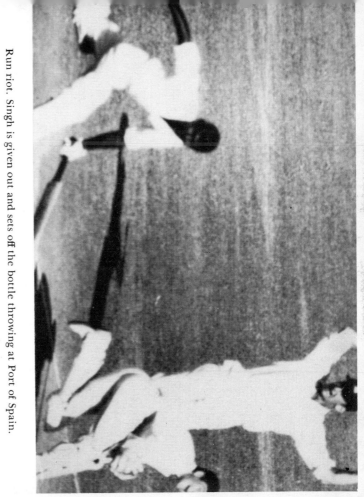

Run riot. Singh is given out and sets off the bottle throwing at Port of Spain.

Neil Harvey attacks from the front foot (*above*). Garfield Sobers makes the same stroke off the back foot (*left*).

Grace and power. Dexter hits powerfully from back stroke (*top*) while Worrell plays the off drive with characteristic fluency (*below*).

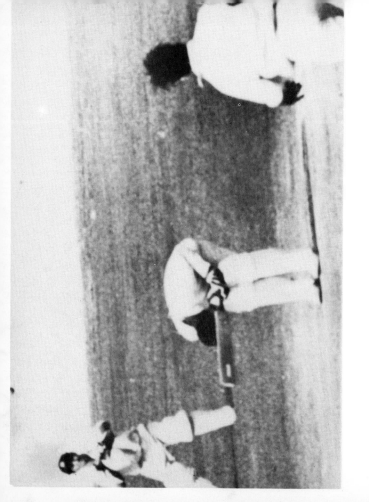

Umpire's view. *Top*—A case for law 46. *Below*—A case for cool judgement.

for it had occurred to many that with the change of circumstances the balance of authority had shifted. Where a captain was new to the job, and indeed a pioneer, it was obvious that greater weight would fall on the shoulders of the manager. It would be necessary to have a man of great fibre and intelligence to guide and discipline the team, for a Test Match cricket side is not composed of non-entities and can contain problem children amongst the older and blasé, or the young and brash. Charles Palmer was not a good appointment for this rôle, solely because of the disarming fault of being too kindly and gentle. While a manager can with advantage be courteous, he must not be self-effacing.

However, the cricket side, after a very bad start in which dreary play led to defeat in the first two Test Matches, went fairly well and the series was unexpectedly drawn.

The next expedition, to Australia, was something of a triumph. It was preceded by some controversy concerning the captaincy, for a section of opinion felt that Sheppard should be appointed in place of the reigning captain. It seemed to others that, apart from any other argument involved, this would place Sheppard in a very awkward position should he be defeated, for there can be no doubt that the deposition of Hutton would have raised a deafening outcry from his admirers who were numerous, and many almost fanatical. Once he was reappointed Hutton had but one bad period. An error of judgement, an understandable one, contributed to overwhelming defeat in the first Test Match at Brisbane and Hutton, a highly-strung and introverted man, was greatly upset. It was uncertain at one time whether he would take the field for the second, but fortunately decided to do so and was there to direct the triumphant fast bowling of Statham and Tyson. From then on his tactics were consistent and successful, if not inspiring.

Hutton may have owed some of his ideas to Bradman, but his philosophy was no doubt profoundly influenced by his early post-war experiences. He had played on a side roundly defeated by Australia and the West Indies and strove to right the balance. Some hardship at the hands of the Australian fast bowlers had certainly confirmed him in his view that this form of attack was the most effective and economical on hard wickets. On his tour in Australia the whole attack was based on the fast bowlers, with relief spells from Appleyard and Wardle. It seemed that Hutton not only directed his quicks to bowl tight but deliberately slowed the whole tempo by leisurely change-overs and frequent conferences. If the Australians disapproved of this they could not escape the fact that Bradman on occasions had done likewise. At any rate it could hardly make for exhilarating batting so, in a war of attrition, the fascination was limited to Statham's consistency and Tyson's terrific pace.

When Hutton retired it did not lead to any great change in policy, for May is a very purposeful cricketer and his tactics are not dissimilar to those of Hutton. In Australia he also based his attack on his fast bowlers and the economical Laker, although it must be admitted he had little choice in the matter. The difference in his leadership, I would say, lies chiefly in a greater willingness to give his batsmen their heads. It is also fair to say that he has made every effort to keep the atmosphere on the field as brisk as is possible; but dependence on up to four fast bowlers inevitably makes for a slow rate of fire.

The recent series in this country against Australia and the West Indies were certainly dominated by spin bowling. But this does not alter the canny spirit of risking as little as possible for, on the receptive pitches provided in these contests, no pair could have been less of a speculation than Laker and Lock. Last season produced some good fast wickets for the matches against India, but here the opposition was too weak to have any great effect on the English tactics; one would surmise that had it been more powerful May would have reverted to his Australian policy.

I have written at some length on the era of Hutton because I believe it has had a great effect on English cricket at top level, and so inevitably on the game as a whole in this country. Once launched on the subject many thoughts arise in the mind.

For instance, the attitude of other countries and how far this is a direct reflection of the leadership. In the case of the Australians Bradman was certainly not a captain to give anything away, but he had a most powerful side and a most acute and active cricket brain. Hassett had less of a side but is a cheerful sanguine character who, even in adversity, is always ready to take a chance. Ian Johnson was a tough determined leader, but in his span had little scope for manoeuvre. Now comes Richie Benaud, a most enterprising player who shows every sign of having the same outlook on captaincy. It must be remarked, however, that on the first threat from May's team he went over to the defensive at a surprisingly early stage. This was, however, thought by many to be the result of powerful pressure from non-playing sources.

Over the period represented by those four captains Australian cricket has on the whole been more positive and aggressive than English. The use of the fast bowlers is in itself indicative.

A fast bowler has a comparatively large margin of pitch which can be described as good length. Now the English fast bowlers all bowl a "good" length but it is commonly at the shorter end of the bracket, where it is normally less dangerous but much more frustrating to stroke play. It is in fact ideal for the patient policy I have ascribed to Hutton and May.

The Australians, Lindwall, Miller, Johnston and Davidson, all bowl a rather fuller length as a general pattern, inviting the batsman to undo himself by playing strokes to the fore. I say general pattern because all fast bowlers drop a bumper from time to time. In the spin department the Australians have not been so strong as in previous years, but they still lean towards the back-of-the-hand spinner, a more erratic type than the orthodox off-breaker or left-hander, but essentially offensive.

123

The South Africans have varied between the splendid and aggressive pace of Heine and Adcock and Goddard's very negative left-handed leg theory so far as the new ball is concerned. Their spinning successes have been Rowan and Tayfield, both from the off but they have had occasional moments with leg-breaks. The South African batting has been similarly varied in character presenting hard, dour facets such as Eric Rowan and McGlew, and occasionally almost reckless enterprise from players like McLean and Winslow. Perhaps what brought South Africa her finest cricketing hour was the fanatical spirit engendered by Cheetham in Australia in 1952-53. One manifestation of this was the most dazzling and determined fielding which did much to draw a series in which the South Africans were accorded no chance at all by the prophets. Here was certainly a very happy example of devoted and inspiring leadership.

In this realm the West Indies' captains, at one period, had comparatively simple tactical problems with which to deal. The powerful, fluent batting order, led by the W's, made plenty of runs at a good pace and, as soon as the shine was off the ball, Ramadhin and Valentine took over. Both being most economical of action and accurate of pitch, they could bowl almost unlimited spells and usually disposed of the opposition with little help from the fast bowlers. In circumstances of such prosperity it may so be that the captain is guided by events rather than the other way about, and this can have an ill effect in later, leaner days. Thus, when the West Indies got into difficulties in Australia it appeared that they lacked the constructive ideas which might have been germinated by a harder apprenticeship. In England in 1957 Goddard was handicapped by the fact that Valentine was through as a Test Match force, but again he could well have made more of his other resources. Not doing so he persisted with Ramadhin to such a degree that eventually that very great bowler was reduced to impotence, even on dusty wickets where Laker and Lock massacred the strong West Indian batting. Goddard is an able cricketer and I would ascribe his limitations as a tactician to lack of early incentive. Percy Fender, most astute of captains, had a naturally inquiring mind; but it was stimulated to constant activity by having to contend with the Oval wickets of the 'twenties, and the most meagre bowling sides. The result was that when given any change of circumstances he was immediate and ingenious, and I remember a professional, who had jogged along under a routine-minded county captain, expressing his delight and surprise at playing with Percy and finding what he was capable of under good direction. It is interesting to speculate in this connection how Warwick Armstrong would have fared as a Test Match captain had things gone hard against him. He had a perfect and evervictorious machine during his reign, but he handled this with a sure touch, and the odds are that he would have been a shrewd, tough tactician in adversity. He had been, of course, a member of losing sides, so learned his craft in a hard school.

Pakistan has been the most successful of the remaining cricketing countries but their play since the partition is a subject which I approach with some caution, bred of ignorance. I have not been to that part of the world since pre-war days and my recollections of Karachi are confined to a dust storm and the vendor of English newspapers who advertised his wares with cries of "Johna da Bull, News of the Next World". When I had the prospect of seeing the Pakistanis play in this country an abominable summer left me with a few hazy watery impressions. Amongst them are several glimpses of Fazal Mahmood bowling a fine leg-cutter that moved very quickly on wet wickets. He was chiefly responsible for the defeat of England at the Oval, but it was in the absence of Bedser on a wicket made for him and the stubborn defence of Bailey, either of whom might have tipped an otherwise nearly balanced scale.

Kardar, who captained Pakistan on that tour and for some seasons after, would seem to be an enigmatical character.

One trait upon which all his opponents are agreed is a great keenness to win, and this, according to tourists, is true of the entire cricket organisation in Pakistan. It is a very laudable attitude up to a point but if over-emphasised can soon be a cause of friction. The M.C.C. team under Donald Carr came in for some censure; but such incidents as ducking an umpire, and unguarded observations on the field were doubtless symptoms of resentment from various causes. Not only the English team but the West Indies have said some pretty harsh things about the standards of umpiring and the facilities for practice and training. Pakistan is a young country and perhaps the next M.C.C. team to visit will find things have progressed to a point where all is joy and peace.

If ever a side called for resolute, cheerful and dynamic captaincy it was the India side of 1959. It was far below the minimum standards of international cricket, and the reason advanced for this state of affairs was that it was a very young side picked with an eye to the future. Now this is a fair policy, but surely the way to implement it is to bring the young ones up in the best and happiest tradition, which is not easy when a side is unequal to its obligations. Experimental or not, it was engaged to meet England in a series of five-day Test Matches. It being plain that this side would be no match for England it would have been much wiser to cast away questions of pride and prestige and go for three Test Matches of three days each. Into these the weaker team can go determined to do or die. There is no disgrace in being beaten provided they have played positively and courageously. With only three days the major side has to keep going to win and the lesser side has always the prospect of a draw, for even if this result should at all times be accidental rather than a target, time is an acknowledged and important ingredient of cricket. I believe that had this been the pattern of events the Indians would have created much interest and acquired a great store of goodwill. As things were, so-called five-day matches more than once came to a premature end, depriving a disgruntled public of a promised day's entertainment. The weaker side, perhaps understandably, adopted negative tactics to prolong the game as far as possible, but only succeeded in achieving a dulling effect on an already foregone conclusion. Eventually the point was reached where, at Manchester, the England captain announced before the start of play that he would not enforce the follow-on so that there could at least be a full Saturday. No wonder many people resent the annual disruption of the County Championship for what is only in name an international series.

The same arguments are in some degree applicable to New Zealand. The New Zealanders come to this country as cricketers, or in any other capacity, with a flying start. Not only are they the smallest Dominion but collectively and individually they are immensely admired and esteemed. The first New Zealand team in 1927 was a great success for it played cricket just as the English public imagined it would. In the 'thirties the New Zealanders undertook the more serious business of playing Test Matches, but there remained the friendly carefree spirit, and three games of three days did little to deprive counties of their leading players.

In 1949 they wanted five days but were only granted four whereat they took the understandable, but surely mistaken, attitude of—if we cannot have five days we shall make sure you don't beat us in four. The result was a dull series.

In 1958 the Test Matches were increased to five days and the results were duller, not to say disastrous. As one of their admirers I would dearly like to see them go back to their original role, and realise to the full the immense reservoir of goodwill they command over here. There would be no surer way of doing so than by adopting the role of a cheerful, lively David against a responsive Goliath. But they must keep slinging, and not longer than three days.

I set out in this chapter to discuss modern cricket with

an eye to describing its development, and comparing it to the previous ages I had known. As always on the the subject of this game any theme leads on to others directly and sometimes subtly connected with it. It is then one realises what a comprehensive and complex game it is and why it remains at all times an inexhaustable topic of discussion. There are a myriad of more detailed points which occur to the writer pondering the broad outlines as I have done, of which each one provides the matter for lengthy and absorbing examination but, as I am confined to reasonable limits of space it is necessary to keep to these broader themes and trends.

Reviewing my thoughts on these as I have set them out I arrive at certain conclusions about present day cricket, and find that these are consistent with the ideas put down when embarking on this book.

The first thought is that the various countries have, as one might expect, preserved their distinctive character despite the fact that cricket is more closely intermixed than at any previous time. This does not alter the fact that various particular teams have naturally reflected the personality of the reigning captain. After all he is quite likely to be typical of his nation or race.

Thus the policies of Hutton and May are a projection of Jardine, Wyatt, Allen and Hammond in that English cricket has been sober and purposeful though not necessarily grim or dull. Australian cricket, based to a much greater extent on week-end clubs, is no less purposeful but rather more thrusting. There have, of course, been sparkling stroke players in English sides between the wars; Woolley, Hammond, Hendren, Duleep, Barnett, Compton, to name a few. But the basis of English batting successes has come chiefly from such sober and reliable sources as a mature and responsible Hobbs, Sutcliffe's iron determination, and stout rearguard actions by Maurice Leyland. Australia's main force has been more the ever aggressive, run-seeking batsman. Bradman was unique, but McCabe, Macartney, Ponsford, Kippax, Morris, Miller, Gregory (who averaged seventy-three in one series), and now O'Neill are, or were, all players of the eager restless school.

Nor in that period can I recall any negative or repressive Australian bowler with the exception of Toshack. Their successes have been founded on pace of the attacking type, or back-of-the-hand spin which in its very nature must kill or be killed. They have never had any number of notable quick medium bowlers, whereas England produced a fair number of this type who can bowl defensively on plumb wickets. The only orthodox Australian left hander of top quality since the first war, Bert Ironmonger, was a fierce spinner of the ball. There was no Australian equivalent to Rhodes or Verity.

In the field an Australian team gives a much greater impression of concentrated effort than any other Test Match team. The vociferous appeal is indicative of the taut, dynamic approach of each individual. I cannot see there is anything wrong in this vocal enthusiasm unless, of course, the question at issue is an LBW decision. The point is that not even the superb English fielding side of the early fifties or the South African side which earlier made such a reputation in Australia, quite gave this impression of coordinated zeal. It may, admittedly, be just an impression, but it is a very strong one.

Although the West Indies had some melancholy moments, indeed days, on their last trip the gaiety and ebullience which is the mainspring of cricket was always just below the surface. When they left the field at Birmingham, a very gloomy moment, the cheerful and delightful Collie Smith, who had taken the one wicket to fall in the day, thrust his way to the fore and made an elaborate bow to a most appreciative members' stand. This gaiety is inclined to be temperamental, and when things go wrong depression is very soon indicated by the field and the fielders. At Lord's the general standard at one time was positively ragged. But the West Indians' powers of recovering their natural good humour are immediate. **Elsewhere I have told how George Challenor, who under-**

stood his team like a father, kept his fast bowlers flat out all day by going to each end periodically and alternately and saying how fast the other chap was by comparison. At the moment of writing I am packing for a trip to the West Indies and am confident that I shall see the sort of cricket I believe to be the true West Indian brand. That is to say colourful and cheerful with always just around the corner a hint of broad comedy. To this I shall return later on.

In an earlier chapter I wrote of my first journey to South Africa when very young and remarked on the very good spirit of South African cricket and its relations with the M.C.C. This was also true when they came here in '29 and '35 and certainly when I went there again in 1930-31. South African cricket then seemed to me to be the ideal blend of serious and good play allied to good sense and sportsmanship. I would judge that South African cricket is now a good deal more ambitious and rather more sensitive but they are not alone in this.

Generally speaking the normal standard of modern Test Match cricket is much the same as in the 'thirties. The immediate post-war era was inevitably a lean time in this country but the Australian side of '48 was very powerful. Although the first XI is now very good I doubt whether there is anything like the number of good batsmen in this country as in the 'thirties, for wet summers and bad wickets had a bad effect on English batsmanship. One year of sun and improved pitches has had an immediately beneficial effect and it is to be hoped that both the weather and the trend will continue. It is the English bowlers who have provided the major part of England's victorious efforts in recent years. Tyson and Statham on lively Australian wickets and Laker and Lock on the dust and mud.

For the reasons which I have sought to bring out the tendency, especially in our own cricket, is to play more defensively. Hutton liked what he called the "hard graft" and suspected stroke players. All modern captains tend to shut the batsman up as soon as he gets in and express wonderment that, in the 'thirties, Bradman was *allowed* to make 300 in a day. They argue that with modern field placing and tactics he could have been curbed or, had he persisted, caused to get himself out. Personally I believe that, on the wickets upon which he made his big scores, it was very, very difficult to keep Bradman quiet and, with the modern defensive field and really accurate bowling, he would still have displaced the pattern and ere long regained the initiative. Remember he made a good many runs in post-war days against modern tactics when, any fair judge will tell you, he was a subdued and gentle performer compared to his pre-war capabilities.

This I think it is fair to say. The modern is more defensively minded and pulls in his horns at the first threat of a flowing scoreboard. He does it very well but he has not invented anything new or original. Even before the LBW law was altered, a great help to the negative bowler, everyone knew all about the packed leg side field, but it was looked upon as the last refuge of the craven. That it has a disastrous effect upon cricket as a game of pleasure and a spectacle has always been freely admitted, and, providentially, efforts are being made to stop it.

Someone asked Maurice Tate what he was doing when Bradman reached 200, to which that honest man replied " Still trying to get him out ". The bowler of the 'thirties may have been naïve in trying to get the batsman out long after he was set, but it made for a better game of cricket. Once again one hopes that the 1960s will see a return to more open off-side cricket; for that is where the game's greatest enjoyment is centred for batsman, bowler, fielder, and spectator. And it will be so much the better if the player finds his own way back instead of being driven thence by the legislator.

CHAPTER EIGHTEEN

Timely Arrival

SPORTING EVENTS ARE, LIKE OTHER phenomena, subject to the laws and cycles of nature. The period of harvest and plenty is followed by the lean and fallow, during which man waits and longs for the return of the golden days. And if you think this is a lot of malarky never mind; it fits in very well with what I have to say which happens to be on the subject of Australian cricket.

The Aussies took guard after the War, with a superb team led by Bradman and later by Hassett with bags of batting, and one of the greatest fast bowling combinations of all time carried all before it, the only element lacking being opposition worthy of its steel. But as the cycle progressed (or cycled?) the players aged, and the greatness departed so that there followed a period of lean when, at least from England, there was altogether too much opposition.

It is also a fact of nature that, during such arid times, men brood on the heroes of the past, and sigh for a new hero, scanning the heavens for a sign. Down under, they brooded, sighed and scanned quite some for a number of years, but it now looks as though their prayers have been answered, the sign given and the man to hand.

Norman O'Neill was born in Sydney in February, 1937 and has lived in that virile, thrusting township ever since. Despite a move to attract him to the rival centre of Adelaide it looks as though his future will continue in the place of his birth. His love of cricket is profound, and was implanted at a stage before his conscious memory. His youthful efforts at the creases, both batting and popping, were zealously encouraged and directed by his uncle Ron, a very good club cricketer who played for Glebe South. And here surely is a potent, for the avuncular influence has always been strong amongst the immortals of cricket. Perhaps some day Uncle Ron will take his place with Uncle Pocock and another Uncle who sawed down his own precious bat in order that it might be more manageable in the hands of his small but prodigious nephew Donald. At any rate his efforts were so successful that soon young Norman was in the first eleven of the Kogarah Intermediate School, and making a great name for himself amongst his young contemporaries. Grade cricket followed with varying fortunes and, at eighteen, came his first appearance for New South Wales against South Australia. Again we have the pattern, for here is a true copy of his own particular section of the score sheet:

N. O'Neill b Gregg o.

(Ah, happy omen.—E. Hendren c Mills, b Dennett o—W. R. Hammond b. Gregory o; b. Mailey 1, etc.).

His true merit was soon recognised not least by the said Sir Donald and his progress since then has been almost uninterrupted. There was much surprise when he was omitted from the team to tour South Africa during the season 1957-58, but he took advantage of the absence of the foremost Australian bowlers to lambast the others for a thousand runs in Shield cricket, an all time record. His encounters with May's team started with a 100 in his first match and 105 runs in his first Test Match for once out. In his short career he has caught the imagination of his fellow countrymen to a greater degree than anyone since Bradman himself. In a time of profound depression amongst cricket supporters and promoters in Australia he, like the nightingale " . . . with fresh hope the lover's heart doth fill ". The potion with which he does so is a fine powerful range of scoring strokes and a keen desire to use them.

In style he is rather more in the accepted English mould than of the typical Australian school, standing rather upright and bringing the bat down from a notably straight and full back lift. If one can liken him at this stage to any one of the great in the past, I would say that in physique and method he is most like Hammond and exercises the same immense power from the back position. But he is also like that great man, and most others, in that he is strongly individual. He is a bowler of leg-breaks and a respectable googly which, if it would hardly carry him to the top unaided, has been known to break several awkward partnerships. He is a superb fielder, except possibly in the slips, with a right arm that picks the wicket-keeper off like a cannon shot from the farthest corner of any field.

This last talent gave rise to many rumours of dazzling offers from visiting American baseball talent scouts. It is a game which O'Neill plays extremely well but the legends he himself gently scotched. They apparently sprang from a conversation when he was sixteen with a representative of the Brooklyn Dodgers who in a genial moment made the young lad and a starry-eyed friend a number of baronial but hazy promises of greatness in America which he never reappeared to define or implement; for which omission good on him. As we go to press the subject seems to have been raised again but without much further result.

Rising twenty-two O'Neill is a fine looking young man, blue eyed, brown haired, an eighth of an inch under six foot and stripping around thirteen and a half stone. As may be gathered from these vital statistics he has a good weight of biceps and forearm to manipulate a bat. He can also swing a golf club but refrains from doing so while playing cricket. In fact when asked about his other games and hobbies he replied that all his spare time was spent practising. It is fortunate that his love of cricket is shared by his wife, a very famous athlete in her own right. Before their marriage she was Gwen Wallace, Australia's eighty metres hurdle champion.

Apparently the other woman in his life is his fourteen year old sister, Lorraine, a promising tennis player. When, in the moment of triumph at Brisbane, your special representative suggested that she must be very proud of him the hero smiled shyly, and replied that he didn't know, but that he was certainly very proud of her. This seemed a disarming, not to say reassuring, outlook for one who has had enough publicity and adulation to put many a young head in orbit.

Good on ya, boy.

CHAPTER NINETEEN

Educating the Young

"HAVING PROVIDED THE YOUNG CRICKETER with the requisite preliminaries to prepare him for playing the game, also with a code of the laws, the next step will be to give him the result of more than fifty years experience and actual practice amongst the finest players the country ever saw". So wrote John Nyren, patriarch of all cricket coaches, in his retirement not so very far from Lord's. His benevolent old shade has only a short flight to see his advice translated into reality a hundred and twenty years later at the Lord's Easter Classes for schoolboys.

The classes were started soon after the first war by Mr. Francis Lacey, as he then was, secretary of the M.C.C. As many other flourishing projects the start was modest enough, and the ground staff were more than adequate to deal with the few boys who attended. It was not long before the idea caught on and, by the beginning of the second war, about 200 boys came daily. The arrangements for the pupils were simple, each batting for half an hour and bowling and fielding for a spell if so inclined. The only scientific aid at this time was a contrivance invented, I believe, by Mr. Lacey and in the nature of a cricketing "Iron Maiden of Nuremburg". This, by means of iron bars, confined the back lift of the bat to a strict, not to say restricted, and narrow path, which can seldom have coincided with that of the ball. Otherwise technical problems were solved on the spot, by the wisdom and experience of the staff. There was, for instance, a lad who had every apparent promise yet was clearly unable to fulfil it. A profound study of this baffling state of affairs by Messrs. Findlay and Aird, by then Secretary and Assistant, failed to produce a satisfactory answer so they sought the guidance of that Lancastrian Solomon, Mr. Archie MacLaren.

135

After a scrutiny of no more than two minutes the Oracle pronounced. "This boy," he said, "is a left, not a right hander". The subject being rotated on his axis and re-orientated accordingly, was immediately and immensely improved.

Another Lancastrian giant, Mr. Walter Brearley, con-ducted a bowling class, and was to be seen daily striding breast-forward across the ground like a stalwart pied piper, his charges trotting expectantly behind him. What they learned of the "basic action" I wouldn't know, but they could not fail to see many a spirited demonstration nor hear tell of many a doughty deed. With luck they might even have been given, by way of illustration of their tutor's pristine pace, the alarming instance of the batsman whose boot he struck with such violence that "You could see *blud coom through bookskin*". If any pupil acquired no more than Walter's enthusiasm, he deserved to play for England.

There was an equally devoted volunteer in a certain Mr. Routledge, a school master from Salop who spent his holiday supervising the nets. As he visited all fifteen in the course of each half hour every day, it is a conservative guess that he walked a distance from Lord's to Bramall Lane and back again every vacation.

The age group lay between 11 and 17 and, naturally, within these margins there was much variation in shape and size. Readers of my generation may recall a young man named Hunter, a somewhat remarkable figure in the Metropolitan Police Force and later the R.A.F. He boxed for England against Golden Glove's team from America at six foot ten, and something over nineteen stone. When he came to Easter classes, aged fourteen, he was some inches over six feet, and a good head and shoulders above his coach, the redoubtable Bill Reeves. It was not un-natural that Mr. Aird, on his rounds, should pause in wonderment at the spectacle of this mountainous figure towering over all about. His fears of optical illusion were abated by Old Bill, who paused in the act of delivering the next ball: "It's all right, sir", he explained, "The boy's queer—Dad's come instead."

They were, as perhaps one may gather, happy, carefree days and, no doubt, highly beneficial in many cases. The same easy system prevailed for some years after the war, but recently the arrangements have been thoroughly over-hauled and, in popular parlance, "streamlined".

The age groups remain the same but instead of the half hour batting, followed by the more or less please-yourself bowling and fielding, there is now a closely scheduled course. This lasts three days and is fairly intensive, in-cluding batting, bowling, fielding in practical form, aug-mented by theory in the shape of films and lectures. The standard of instruction is high, as almost every coach holds the M.C.C. coaching certificate and teaching is thus more uniform. No longer can the Lord's staff provide sufficient tutors, so that it is now necessary to bring in outside help. There are many good cricketing names on the roster, though their fame belonged to a day before the arrival of their charges. Jim Sims and Len Muncer are happy in their old home. Fred Price looks after the up and coming wicket keeper, and the manly and magnificent figure of Bill Voce stands where once did Walter Brearley, midst the Barneses and Bedsers of the future. In passing, one may say they need not grieve if those charges wot not of them —the author of an absorbing book I have just read on Jutland was prompted to write it on meeting a midship-man who had never heard of the battle.

There is no restriction regarding the entrants as to school or creed or domicile but, the places being con-sistently over-subscribed, preference is given to sons of members. The figures in fact are roughly 600 applicants for 450 places. All entrants' forms must be endorsed by their games master to the effect that the entrant has some ability and a genuine interest in the subject, which again is a very reasonable precaution. For there must be a very strong temptation amongst harassed parents to see the

young hopeful completely, and perhaps gainfully, employed for three whole days whether he likes it or not.
There is also the over-ambitious father who is determined
his son will succeed whatever his feelings. Thus, despite
these precautions the occasional black sheep or heretic does
turn up; as the other day when a young gentleman suffered
a very slight blow on the knee at which he announced his
retirement from the course. To his coach's somewhat
scathing comments he replied, with perfect aplomb, that
he understood there was a long waiting list, and that he
loathed the rotten game anyway. But the vast majority are
filled with a great enthusiasm which brings them from
considerable distances; from as far North as Glenalmond
in Perthshire and as far South as Queen Victoria College
in Jersey. This enthusiasm is reciprocated by staff and
officials alike and even a razor-edged East wind did little to
lessen the interest of instructor or the eagerness of instructed when your correspondent called to see the young
and renew his youth, at least in mind.

Only in one quarter did he encounter any disapproval.
Peter is a figure famous and respected as being, amongst
other things, the only cat to bring a Test Match to a halt,
which he did by the simple expedient of taking station
behind the bowler's arm and refusing to move. In an ex-
clusive interview by his cosy fireside he indicated that,
like all other summertime intrusions, the classes interfered
with his pigeon stalking.

CHAPTER TWENTY

The Hand of the Bowler

WHILE FEW, LIKE HOLMES, CAN TELL a man's craft from a glance at his hands, most cricketers would be able to tell a spin bowler's methods from a look at his. The seam bowler suffers very much less wear and tear to his fingers and, as a rule, bears little evidence of his toil. It is, however, the spinner with whom we are concerned.

It cannot be said that his hand is the most important part of a spin bowler's equipment, any more than it can be said that a wheel is the most important part of a car, but a good hand for the job is an absolute essential, for it is its dexterity which eventually determines the finer margins of length and direction and arms or fuses the ball.

There is no standard pattern of hand among the great spinners I have seen. Naturally, there has been a great variety of size and shape of hand, and these characteristics do not seem to be of paramount importance. Suppleness and flexibility of finger, of course, are common to all. Thus Gupte and Ramadhin, although they have the small, delicate hands of their race, comparable in size with those of Freeman, have a good span and can comfortably grip and spin the ball.

At the other end of the scale Tom Goddard has an immense hand. But the first prize for size in this century must go to Dave Nourse senior, one of the great characters of South African cricket. Aubrey Faulkner used to say that when Albert Trott, who was said to have the biggest hands of any spinner in England, was introduced to old Dave his hands looked quite lady-like in that massive grasp. Nourse was not one of the great spinners, and may indeed have been handicapped by the very massiveness of his grasp; for trying to spin a cricket ball must have been as tricky to him as spinning a golf ball to the normal hand. Another case of the would-be spinner being embarrassed by outsize fingers was that of Jack Durston who was the biggest man with whom I ever played cricket. He was bothered for some years when bowling fast by an injury to his elbow which prevented him from fully straightening his arm, and eventually the time came when he decided to experiment with the gentler art of the off-spinner. One of his early appearances in this rôle was on a wet dull day at Bradford with Herbert Sutcliffe going great guns. I remember the occasion clearly for Walter Robins and myself officiated as backward and forward short legs respectively, standing at the customary very short range. All went well for the first few balls but, having found his length, the bowler then decided to give the ball a really vicious tweak. The net result was that the slippery ball shot out of that vice-like grip as a soap or an apple pip to a towering height, an accident fortunately reflected by the expectant expression in the batsman's upturned countenance. Despite this ample warning he had some difficulty in getting his short legs to keep station, after this had occurred thrice in one over.

These outsizes do, of course, border on the realm of freakdom where belongs another left hand, Bert Ironmonger of Victoria and Australia. He is a picturesque character, said to be the worst batsman, and, on no less authority than that of Pat Hendren, the best left-hand bowler of his time.

A considerable portion of his spinning finger is missing and legend says it was removed in two instalments. The first on being thrust experimentally into the teeth of a circular saw, and the second on its owner demonstrating to a bystander what had happened in the first instance. At any rate the stump proved itself a first-rate implement, and batsmen describe how the ball used to hum as it came through the air.

His one-time contemporary O'Reilly, who was by general consent the best of the spinners between the wars, and has not since been rivalled, has a large hand in perfect proportion to a large man. He again always seems free from any finger troubles, but it is fair to say that he was not a fierce spinner of the ball, except where his wrong 'un was concerned.

Arthur Mailey, who probably spun the ball more than anyone before or since, certainly since, has a hand of normal size but immensely strong, rather spatulate fingers. These characteristics he attributes in his life story to an apprenticeship as a glass-blower.

Grimmett, who succeeded as Australia's chief leg-spinner, still has a bowl in his own garden from time to time just for the joy of it all. His hands are normally sized for a smallish man but, like the rest of him, flexible and durable. They were not only deft and sensitive but connected to a very alert, calculating mind. I can remember discussing the intricacies of spinning with Clarrie thirty years ago in an Oxford hotel. He summed the whole matter up by saying, "It is all in the position of the hand." He then, with much enthusiasm, demonstrated the subtle alterations in manipulation that give him the wonderfully graduated scale of spin from leg-break through top-spinner to genuine googly.

The greatest spin-bowler of all, Sydney Barnes, has manly but not abnormally large hands. Many is the time I have surreptitiously slipped a ball into that supple, dexterous grasp for the pleasure of seeing the still sure touch. It is also a treat to see its owner's eye light up as he lets the ball roll from his palm into an immensely firm hold between the first three fingers (as he used to do at the end of his run). A flexible snap and the ball buzzes out as for the quick leg-break. I never heard that he suffered from split fingers, and his hands have no permanent calluses, although presumably he must have developed them when fully active.

It is likely that Laker will carry the marks of his successes through the years. The off-spinner and the orthodox left-hander throw almost the whole strain of propulsion on to the index finger at the moment of delivery and this must be considerable. In Laker's case an otherwise normally shaped and sized hand is conspicuous for a very swollen and bent index finger. It is said to fill medical men with awe and alarm, and an X-ray made in Australia was regarded as a prize piece. Apart from the tension on the muscles and ligaments there is also the damage caused by friction to the skin and here Laker is probably more fortunate than his fair-skinned opposite, Lock, who has a certain amount of trouble with his spinning finger. A naturally tender skin he hardens by the application of surgical spirit to keep his fingers in trim.

Keeping the fingers in trim is quite a problem, and is peculiar to the bowler himself. Walter Robins, a ferocious spinner of the ball, used to doctor a raw third finger with sticking-plaster, but this is rather liable to interfere with a bowler's touch. At the other end I was much troubled with blood blisters and splits just by the nail of my first finger, and after much experiment found it best to keep the skin shaved thin and fairly soft. I remember recommending this course to Valentine, the West Indian, who had an immense corn inside his spinning finger which had split down the middle, and seemed to me to have little prospect of healing. If he was a shade dubious, it was doubtless a lack of confidence in my medical experience rather than any suspicion of sabotage.

Lastly, a couple of pairs of hands any leg-spinner, however devoutly raised, must covet. They belong to the brothers Bedser, and are shapely but enormous and powerful. Eric, being an off-spinner, has a little trouble with his index finger. Alec, on being asked if his leg-cutter, which is nearing the realm of spin, caused any abnormal wear and tear, said he had no trouble. His hands, he said, were good and strong. But, he added, in view of Surrey's progress on the improved wickets of 1959, what was more important was that so were his feet.

CHAPTER TWENTY-ONE

Scoreboard

WHEN I WAS VERY YOUNG I WAS BIDDEN, DURING a Test Match at Manchester, to dine with the Jam Sahib of Nawanagar. The host, as you may remember, when himself young had achieved a certain measure of fame and success as K. S. Ranjitsinhji.

The only other member of the side or of my generation present was his nephew, Duleep, and we were somewhat overawed by the august body of England captains and illustrious names which assembled around us. All, especially the host, were extremely kind and the dinner was the best that Manchester's foremost hotel could provide, so that the evening was a great success and, to us youngsters, an event. But the conversation, which I clearly remember, inclined to one main theme. It was that cricket was a great game, how well it used to be played and what a pity it was that it was now dying, as nobody could play it any more.

There was an ironical sequel the following day when someone produced an ancient yellow newspaper cutting which recorded an interview with Prince Ranjitsinhji, just after his brilliant first appearance for England in 1896. He was reported as saying that he hoped that, when the years had carried him past playing days and into retirement, he would be a more lenient critic of the succeeding generation than his elders were of his.

It is a memory I always try to recall before making any criticism of modern players for one's recollection of one's own times are inclined to become ivy clad. Every sport measurable in absolute terms has improved with the passage of time and it is probable that games, to which no yardstick is applicable, have also developed. It is, however, possible that, for various reasons, the development may take a wrong turn and many people, including my-self, believe that this has occurred in English cricket and that the game has lost much of its attraction and, outside its home grounds, its efficiency.

To judge from the general attitude encountered on re-turning from Australia, English cricket had not received such an unexpected rebuff as the recent 4-0 defeat since Armstrong rolled massively over the inflated reputation of Douglas's 1920-21 side. In almost every detail the circumstances are very different, but there is a great simi-larity between the incredulity of the twelve-year-old Scots supporter, with whom we started, that cricketers existed who could so manhandle his heroes, and the dumb pain of the English enthusiast whose (metaphorical) posterior hit the earth with such a bump.

The cause of this painful experience was of course the cricketing fool's paradise in which we had lived for some time. Its roots lay in the past. In the 'thirties pitches in England achieved what, from their creators' point of view, was a state of perfection. On the other hand the bowler shorn of all aid could hardly be expected to share in the general satisfaction. But there was some entertainment to the spectators in the spectacle of Bradman, Hutton or McCabe thrashing the naked trundler with whips and scorpions for, if it contained something of the cruelty and inevitability of a bull-fight, it could claim similarly beauti-ful moments. However, when the novelty of records had worn off this extreme, like most others, grew tedious and piteous cries were raised on behalf of the bowler. Just as a start he was given a rather more helpful LBW rule, but this was very slight assistance, and availed him but little as scores still mounted until England topped 900 in 1938.

In the early post-war years people were so grateful to see cricket again that it was a little time before the faults of inflated scores again became apparent. At this point a ministering angel rushed to the aid of the bowler. Rather a surprising one; for it was his old persecutor, the grounds-man, who, having put by his pail of dope and locked up his heavy roller, now provided some nice loose, abrasive surfaces, presumably by the judicious use of his spiked tail and cloven hooves.

What with the added help of a succession of wet summers the ball was soon turning merrily on the first day and the batsman reduced to a nervous prodder or a reckless swinger. It was very gratifying to see strong sides from overseas roundly defeated as their wickets fell like ninepins, but the actual play soon became as tedious as the inflated scores of the 'thirties. And the trend in this case was much more harmful; for it is a thoroughly bad training ground for batsman and bowler alike.

Batsmen from overseas, accustomed to their own very different pitches, took all this very ill indeed and were inclined to hint that it was a very " happy accident " that we had produced these pitches when we had the finest spinning combination (on faulty surfaces) in the world. To these thinly veiled accusations—and some weren't veiled at all—I was wont to reply that these were typical English pitches of the era and, even if they were not wholly accidental they were an honest, but misguided, attempt to hold the balance between bat and ball, and not a ruthless conspiracy to entrap the trusting guest.

This I believe to be true, but the sad thing is that any thinking person has always known that this is the last way to enliven the game. The effects were as expected. The science of batting was handicapped by uncertainty and stroke play consequently stultified. The greatest virtue that a bowler could have is economy, so that nothing is given away before the inevitable departure of the struggling batsman. Close fielding may have been sharpened to the point of brilliance but otherwise one is reminded of Alec Bedser's mot that the English fielders don't throw so well for nobody at present hits the ball far enough to give them any practice.

The effects of these trends were plain to see when our team was confronted with the fast, true Australian wickets. Only three batsmen ever looked like Test Match players.

BOWLER'S TURN

The fast bowlers did nobly, and in passing one should say a word about their place in recent English cricket history. Very good they are, but in only one major series have they been decisive—under Hutton's captaincy in 1954-55. On very lively and occasionally unruly Australian wickets the glorious accident of Tyson tipped an otherwise balanced scale. I say accident because his selection was acknowledged to be a calculated risk, and his immense development due to a great change in technique well on in the tour. It must be borne in mind that while Statham and Tyson performed magnificently and without interruption, Australia seldom had Miller and Lindwall in action together, and that Lindwall was past his best. On the next fast wicket provided for an English v. Australia match at Lord's in 1956, Miller was the decisive fast bowler. It may be safely said that England's spinners, not the fast bowlers, put their side in its dominant position which it has occupied in this country during the past five years.

In Australia when the fast bowlers had done there was no suitable spin bowling to take over, for Laker's success was due to his superb craftsmanship, learnt on good wickets; but his type of bowling would have met with scant success in lesser hands. Our fielding once again lagged far behind the tremendous standard set by the Aussies and this, with the other shortcomings I have described, was a nasty shock to those accustomed to our string of victories on home pitches.

I have written these strictures in the past tense because one season, 1959, of sun and better wickets worked wonders for English batsmanship and will do for English bowlers if, as we are promised, we had a series of good summers and well made pitches. There is still, however, a good way to go and many problems to be tackled.

Over the years I have acquired a good many ideas on the improvement of cricket, but must admit that in view of fairly recent developments some of them call for revision. For a start I have always upheld the alteration of the LBW rule and indeed advocated its extension. It has been a tricky law throughout cricket history ever since in early days the legislators inserted a canny clause which said that the batsman was out should he put his leg in the way "with a purpose". When the only protection for the batsman's shins was his silken hose he probably thought twice, even in a hardy age, before facing the umpire with a problem involving thought-reading as well as geometry. But by the time pads had swollen sufficiently to provide complete shock absorption the most craven of strikers could use his legs freely "with a purpose". As it always seemed to me that a ball good enough to beat the bat and hit the stumps deserved a wicket I applauded the widening of the rule to include the off-side. I hoped Bradman's idea to dispense with the clause concerning the leg being in a line between wicket and wicket would be adopted.

Now my opinion has wilted before the monotonous spectacle of in-swingers and off-spinners driving the play towards a packed on-side field. Let us therefore return to the old rule and, to mitigate to some extent its inherent injustice, widen the wicket at least to the point where a fast bowler of high action can pitch on and hit the wicket with a straight good-length ball. R. E. S. Wyatt, a profound thinker on such matters, advocates a fourth stump, but here I take issue on aesthetic grounds. Three stumps have a certain symmetrical beauty, but any more would look like a five-barred gate. Anyway, think of the cricket writer wrestling with the "inside off" or the "outside leg" whenever the castle was struck.

Further discouragement to dreary on-side tactics should be given by making the experimental limitations of the on-side field general law.

One particularly damping feature of modern cricket, especially in international sides, is anything up to four fast bowlers on the same side. One fast bowler is a fine inspiring spectacle, two may be company, but any more is a crowd, or rather a mob, and at times in Australia with spells of fast bowlers, all running upwards of eighteen yards, the rate of fire dropped to fifteen overs (eight balls) an hour.

One also has the impression that habits on the field have changed. Looking to yesteryear one sees in the mind's eye Lol Larwood marching briskly back to the end of a sixteen-yard run to the strains of the "Washington Post". Now the fast bowler lumbers back twenty-eight yards, head bent, shoulders bowed, to the sombre tempo of "The Volga Boat Song", punctuated by sarcastic inquiries from the Hill as to whether he has lost a loved one. (Possibly I have stumbled on a new field for investigation. If incidental music would help to accelerate the proceedings I would even settle for Tommy Steele — in short bursts.) The real answer to this problem is very difficult to find, but one would hope that on fast wickets other and less ponderous forms of attack, such as leg-spinners, would gradually supplant the massed batteries beloved of Napoleon and modern captains.

In fact the one condition essential to all these suggestions is that every effort is made to produce fast true wickets. To this end the present experiments with covering pitches are all to the good and the practice might well be extended. As I have previously argued, many of our troubles, and the dullness of much of our cricket, can be ascribed to dusty and muddy wickets. If and when runs become over-plentiful it will be time to consider some logical means of adjusting the balance. But it must not be at the expense of the stroke player.

After an age of superb fielding England has again receded in this department and is now obviously inferior to Australia in every respect. This I would attribute to one of the first causes of all our troubles, which is that we try to play too much cricket.

It may be said that the summer programme is no greater than in pre-war days. But circumstances have changed a great deal. Amateurs are rare in times when harsh economics have extinguished even the temporary gentleman of leisure. The steep rise in wages and salaries has lessened the attraction of cricket as a career, with its element of risk, while the great increase in the strength of certain Commonwealth countries puts an immense and increasing demand on our limited number of top players. These and less tangible factors war against attractive domestic cricket at a time when, if cricket is to hold its own unaided by supporters' clubs, it must out-rival an enormously increased amount of counter-attraction.

Ideally, cricket would be confined to week-ends, but here one runs head-on to the vexed question of Sunday sport. This is not the place for theological controversy, but if ever the various parties were reconciled and week-end cricket established the benefits to the game would be enormous. Practically all players would be available for first class cricket and would be always at concert pitch. Additionally, from the spectator's point of view, anyone who wanted to follow his side would have a good chance of seeing the start and the finish of the match. A certain amount of mid-week cricket would be sustained by touring teams, Test Matches and other special occasions.

All these reflections are directed at the "end product", so to speak, and some may argue that in trying to revitalise cricket this is rather putting the cart before the horse, and that early opportunity and training is the place to look. I am inclined to disagree on two grounds—first, that it is largely the performance in leading strata that sets the standards of keenness and efficiency of the game as a whole; second, that, led by the M.C.C. and the counties, many bodies are devoted to training youth on sound lines. All that is required is expansion and development of their efforts, and this is largely a question of finance. The great point is that when the players have arrived there should be ample scope for their talents at the top and that they are not, as so often at present, lost to the game.

My only technical observations on teaching and training would be to teach them on fast true surfaces to hit the ball first and learn to defend later. (All the great I have seen were fiercely attacking players in their youth.) To bowlers I would say learn to spin first and learn control once you have mastered the mechanics of your craft. To all—learn to field and throw. If you are so blessed that you can eventually throw like Norman O'Neill you will not only enjoy every moment in the field but will give limitless pleasure to everyone present — except perhaps the scurrying batsmen.

It is nonsense to say that cricket is a dying game, as one so often hears. It is far too good a game ever to die as long as Britons draw breath. Probably more people play and follow cricket in this country than ever before—but it is no longer the sole summer entertainment. On beaches, mountains, roads, cruising liners and lidos you will find cricket-lovers who a generation ago, lacking the means and facilities now available, might have gone to a cricket match. They are not necessarily less interested than their parents but they have cars to take them into the country and television on which they can see the chief events of the day's play. And there are far more people playing in the world than thirty years ago.

All this is not to say that first class and international cricket has not struck a dull era and that unless it can offer a good deal more attraction it might well shrivel to a very minor position in the scale of international sport. This would be a lamentable state of affairs. When 100 runs in a day is the average tally there is still an air of combat, especially where England and Australia are concerned, but this is not sufficient to attract the average spectator day after day. When the spirit of combat is allied to eventful play international cricket is the best of the game and to many the best of all games.

With the M.C.C. in the West Indies

With the M.C.C. in the West Indies

Barbados

Trinidad

Jamaica

Georgetown, British Guiana

Back to Trinidad

Test Averages

THE M.C.C. SIDE TO THE WEST INDIES SET OUT in a somewhat different spirit to that which had surrounded its predecessor to Australia in the previous winter. The public regarded the latter as a great side assured of success, despite the misgivings of the thoughtful who pondered the difference between hard Australian wickets and the dusty or muddy wickets upon which so many home Test Matches had been won. Events proved the doubters right, and the shortcomings bred of these pitches came painfully to light.

There were no such high-flown hopes of the greatly changed side which Peter May led to the West Indies. The changes were mainly of young, comparatively inexperienced players for well-tried veterans, and there was some dubiety as to how they would fare against the great strength of a West Indian side on its own pitches. The verdict of those who followed it first hand was that the trip was a major success in every respect. Its cricket record was outstandingly good, its behaviour exemplary, and its drawing power sufficient to fill the coffers of the deserving, but not over rich, West Indian Board of Cricket.

The general pattern of the cricket was of matches played on over perfect wickets where the batsmen dominated the proceedings. To my taste it is not an interesting form of cricket, although admittedly better than that on "sporting wickets". But the brutal truth is that the only really positive and effective weapon the bowler has is the bouncer or very fast short ball directed at the batsman, and when this is exploited to the full cricket is not a very edifying spectacle. Upon seeing it I wrote to the *Sunday Times* as follows:

"Once again we have had a sustained and persistent bout of short pitched bowling interspersed with all too frequent bouncers from the home side, and some retaliation from the English fast bowlers. I do not regret this reply, for although mild in comparison it may draw the attention of the recipients to the fact that aunt sally is not really much of a game when one finds oneself in the role of aunty.

It may also bring matters to a pitch where some temporary agreement on the subject can be reached. I say temporary, for very soon something very decisive of a permanent nature must be done to rule this evil out. It is the absolute ruination of decent cricket as a game, as a spectacle and as an oft quoted model of fair play.

All the major cricketing powers have at one time or another transgressed, while the others, who have had to endure the bully at the moment in the ascendancy, have bided their time until the day he is exhausted and they have had the means of retaliation. And so it is likely to go on until really positive action is taken to prevent it.

The origins of this form of intimidation, for that is what it is, are largely to be found in over perfect pitches. Doped wickets led to body-line bowling, and it is patent in the present series that the complete ineffectiveness of the respectable seamer or spinner diverts the fast bowling to this, the one potent weapon.

Even with this form of attack freely used the average number of wickets to fall in a day seldom exceeded four, and this became very tedious after a time. The reader may well say that I grumble at bad wickets and also at good ones—just what do I want? My answer is that for years I have pleaded for an even balance between bat and ball and that this can only be achieved by making the best possible wickets and then devising a ball that will swing and turn a little on them. This should be perfectly possible and anyone who has seen this balance achieved, as on good matting wickets, will know that there is never any occasion for dull play and cricket is a game of sustained interest and excitement." These views remain unaltered on reviewing the tour as a whole after due time for reflection.

For May the trip brought success as a captain, but sadness

154

and disappointment as a man and a player. It was only at a late stage that the true reason for his non-success as a player came to light, when it was learnt that the wound left by his operation was not properly healed. He must have suffered great pain and inconvenience, and might have been well advised to give up at an earlier stage. But he is not a man to give up, especially where he considers his duty to his side is concerned. Eventually his hand was forced and, when the situation was known, all who doubted his judgement could not but admire his fortitude.

He has his critics, as all captains, and their objections are chiefly directed at his caution and inflexibility as a tactician. One can only say that his tactics worked and, especially in the Trinidad Test, critics who voiced disapproval were frequently confounded in the next moment. As a batsman he was vulnerable to the bouncer; but it takes a very fit man indeed to cope with this ball as bowled by Watson and Hall.

For Brian Statham, the head professional, the tour also ended sadly when, after a week's unrelieved anxiety, he flew back to his ailing son. I would guess he is too amicable and easy-going to make an effective authority, but he must be one of the most useful and amenable bowlers any captain has had at his command. He seems prepared to bowl his best at any time from either end as long as required, and his best can still be pretty good. At Trinidad he gave an exhibition of seam bowling with a worn ball I have seldom seen equalled. How long his span has to go is difficult to estimate because of a most abnormal suppleness which exempts him from the ordinary standards of wear and tear.

Having got on to the subject of bowling one may as well complete a brief survey of this department. Trueman bowled splendidly throughout the trip and, day in, day out, was the spearhead. He may not be quite as fast as of yore but he bowled with fine control and unflagging spirit. His best spell brought him but two wickets and was bowled at Georgetown when he yorked Walcott and beset Worrell for several overs, without actually getting his wicket.

The third paceman, Moss, was willing but unsuited in speed and technique to the wickets he encountered. He is a good bowler in England, not by virtue of sheer pace, but by good seam work and this has few opportunities in the West Indies. In the absence of Rhodes it is very difficult to think of any English bowler who would fill the bill.

With wickets of great perfection completely protected from the weather the spinner's lot is not a happy one. The only response he will get, until maybe a few spots on the last day or two, is in the rough made by his colleagues' feet. Accuracy, flight and stamina are the only ingredients of success and there is little positive action to be taken against resolute batting. Here Allen and Barrington both did very well in their respective styles and Illingworth was a most useful stop-gap, given the melancholy assumption that it was not his business to get wickets. Neither Dexter nor Greenhough were successful for, despite their widely differing styles, their common fault was lack of control to the required margins. Both are profound students of their subject and immensely enthusiastic so it is to be hoped that success will eventually attend their efforts; although in Dexter's case it is of small consequence against the brilliance of his batting.

When one considered the doubts voiced at the time of his selection, Dexter was the outstanding success amongst the batsmen. At a great disadvantage in being a late-comer, he gave little sign of promise in Australia. Another trip to that Dominion would, I am certain, be a vastly different story. Against every type of bowling in the West Indies he was a superb stroke player, dealing with the tempestuous quickies with a majestic command which visibly damped their boyish enthusiasm. His two hundreds in Tests in Barbados and Georgetown were an unalloyed joy even in a monotonous type of cricket.

Cowdrey has still got reservations about opening the innings, which is strange, for he must be the best number one in the world. He has the full equipment and at times he needed it. Latterly he took guard on middle and off in order to better his chances of hooking, and it seemed that when he did so he also took some of the danger and certainly a good deal of the ardour out of the fast bowlers. No one since Compton has swung a bat with such a pleasing mixture of ease and momentum, nor seen the ball fly out of it more sweetly.

He was most ably supported by Geoff Pullar, a fine solid left-handed Lancastrian and a real character. Both in their different ways met the fast bowler extremely well and they must, on present form, be the most successful English opening pair, certainly since Hutton and Washbrook, maybe since the immortal Hobbs and Sutcliffe partnership. With his ability, physique and temperament Pullar should have a pretty good future.

Mike Smith had a chequered career. He played well and indeed most gracefully when started, but seemed to have difficulty in picking up the line of the fast half volley or yorker in the first few overs. Barrington played several heroic innings. He obviously disliked the continuous short fast bowling, as well he might, but stuck it out. He is now a very fine all-round cricketer.

Subba Row was a success, and when the chance came he seized it. It struck me on the Australian trip he was one of the more promising players against the pace attack and this was borne out when he faced the West Indians. He looked a fine solid performer on all occasions.

Allen was the best of the later batsmen and it was surprising how long it was before he was promoted in the order. Trueman offered some resistance, but after the first Test, Swetman was always overwhelmed by Hall or Watson's pace. Statham has always been a beautiful but unambitious hitter of the ball, and did some useful service in his chosen place.

Swetman was preferred to Andrew as a wicket keeper but when the former failed as a batsman there cannot be a great margin in his favour. Parks, who joined the side at

Georgetown with resounding success, is surely the best proposition, with his ability as a batsman. If he is to be the
regular choice it greatly extends the batting order, and gives
much greater latitude in the selection of the bowlers.

In general it may be said that the team was worked up
from a collection of young, comparatively raw, international
players with a leavening of experience, to a very well organised team. Its spirit was manifested on several occasions
when collapse threatened but recovery was effected quite
late in the day. The same spirit was apparent through
many testing spells in the field, when the fielding was always first-class and the bowling unflagging. The future at
the moment looks very good.

The West Indies, with much individual talent, never
seemed to achieve the same degree of concerted effort. They
have some beautiful batsmen, two really fast opening
bowlers and some good spin in Ramadhin, Singh, Scarlett
and Gibbs, to say nothing of Sobers' variable chinamen.
Perhaps a tour to Australia will weld the various com-
ponents into a really well constructed machine.

Much credit for the success of the trip must go to
Walter Robins who, by common consent, was a most remarkable mixture of tact, firmness, brimstone, understanding, mustard and enthusiasm. He handled several
delicate situations with unfailing aplomb, and dealt with
the conflicting interests of players, press, public, hostesses
and dignitaries to the satisfaction of all—or as near to it as
human imperfection will allow.

In the following pages I have attempted to give a brief
picture of the cricket as played in each island.

158

BARBADOS IS AN ISLAND ROUGHLY THE SIZE of the Isle of Wight with a population of about 220,000. So deep are the roots of cricket, however, that Barbados regularly produces a side of a strength quite disproportionate to these modest dimensions. The roots have had time to reach wide and deep, for Barbados were playing against their neighbours of Demerara a hundred years ago, from which time they have bred a series of players whose names are world famous, and who have brought the gaiety and sunshine of their island to the game wherever they have travelled. Challenor is a name which was placed close to Hobbs by all who saw him in his heyday, and is still revered by a generation, most of whom never saw him play at all. In passing I may say that I played against him but once, and had the mortification of dropping him in the slips first over. At that he laughed and made light of my blunder so that I felt much better, buoyed up by the gaiety of spirit so vividly reflected in his play.

Within two years of each other and within the same parish were born the three W's, the dominating trio of their times. The one factor common to their batting was its superlative quality. Otherwise one of the fascinations of this comradeship in arms was that each member was so intensely individualistic. The powerful, dominating Walcott, the flowing, sinuous Worrell and the strong, stocky Weekes. Which, if any, was the greatest has ever been a matter of argument and opinion without definite conclusion; but many bowlers who have suffered from all three incline to put Weekes as the toughest proposition in all circumstances. This may well be an accurate judgement, but the probability is that each had his moments of ascendancy, although these were hard to discern in the general brilliance of the company.

The perfect pitches which bred, or certainly matured, such batsmen would hardly seem to offer great inducement to the young bowler, but have produced Francis and Martindale, both of whom did yeoman service. Martindale in his prime was amongst the really fast, with the bounding, wheeling action borne of great strength and elasticity. In the same mould is Wesley Hall, the fastest of all at the moment of writing and a magnificent prospect. He still has something to learn about control but, with his high action and exceptional pace, must be a fearsome prospect on anything approaching a lively wicket.

The leading modern Barbadian batsman is, of course, Gary Sobers. He is a most complete and attractive player, whom only Neil Harvey can rival amongst left handers in the present age. He has recently developed as a left handed googly bowler, a type of spin he apparently bowls very well indeed. His true merit in this line is, however, hard to assess on his native pitches, because spin has so little effect upon them. One would judge that in England he would be a very useful support to the main attack.

The ground upon which these smooth and lasting wickets are laid out is the very pleasant one of Bridgetown. The island having a plentiful supply of water the outfield is lush and green, with a thick crop of grass of similar type and quality to the couch of Australia. On the pitch itself very little grass is visible at all, the surface being of clay and rolled to the texture of marble. A six-day match makes little impression and what wear there is is almost instantly repairable, and the strip ready for immediate re-preparation.

The ground will accommodate 12,000 spectators besides the members, this number being roughly divided in half between stands and open space. The open space is caged in by wire netting, a precaution which seemed outdated for the Barbadian crowd, although lively to English standards, is staid to those of the West Indies. They are nonetheless gay and, if absolutely absorbed by the events of the play, always welcome a little extraneous entertainment.

This they derive in good measure from a local character named "King" Dyall, whose sartorial tastes would have made Beau Brummell look drably colourless. His suits are elegantly tailored in bright red, yellow, sky blue and other shades long deprecated in Saville Row and the City, quarters in which his somewhat incongruous accessories, consisting of Homburg hat and furled umbrella, would do little to redress the adverse balance. His arrival, always studiously timed, is the signal for a cordial and noisy welcome.

It was against this background that May led out his young and largely experimental team on the first season's match of their tour. There was not in fact a very great crowd present, but this was attributed to the fact that it was a working day, and that many of the cognoscenti were saving their dollars for the Test Match, as to most the price of admission, and a modest capital for sporting investment, meant a considerable outlay. May lost the toss and very soon every English bowler must have felt rather as though he were some material or article saddled to a machine designed to test it to bursting point. Pitted against a massive batting order it was early apparent that there was no help to be expected for seam or spin, and that accuracy, patience, faith and a long term belief in human fallibility was the only recipe for taking wickets. Two great individual innings went to carry the score to the final majestic figure of 513 for five wickets. A slim young right hander named Nurse showed a fine freedom and variety of strike from the first over he received, and continued to do so until he had made 213. Sobers soon demonstrated that the injury to his hand had at least recovered to a point where it in no way impeded him, and made some glorious strokes in scoring 154. When these two batted together it was, if rather one-sided, sparkling cricket. But for my taste, when the bowler is shorn of all the weapons with which he seeks to take the initiative and the score inexorably swells, the most dazzling sparks become monotonous, and the eye loses its zest. So it was in this case and I longed to see the ball jump or turn. Wistful thoughts of an occasional dead shooter I sought to dismiss as unworthy.

When eventually the M.C.C. batted against, in the absence of Hall, a fairly moderate Barbados bowling side the results were disappointing. Pullar made a capital impression as an opener, Barrington lived up to his comparatively recent reputation as a fully fledged England batsman, and Dexter looked a very different player from his uncertain Australian days; but a total of 238 was meagre indeed. The follow-on was slightly more promising. Cowdrey and May both got in some useful practice, Barrington made another 79 and Illingworth made 72 of a total of 352. This set Barbados 58 to win in 28 minutes and Hunte and White put their heads down and charged. Rain fell heavily for most of the time which materially aided their progress, and the last 45 runs came off five overs. It was a grandstand finish and May's generosity in staying out and keeping the tempo as brisk as possible was greatly acclaimed. It was indeed a very happy finish.

The lesson which arose from this match was that the M.C.C. were not as yet natural fast wicket players, despite our good summer. A man naturally acquires an instinct for the conditions to which he is accustomed and will, without conscious effort do, or aim to do, what is most advantageous to his own particular talent. A Yorkshire cricketer will automatically station himself at the requisite distance from the striker on a soft green field. He will also know the length to bowl on a slow, wet wicket. An Australian cricketer of experience will play the type of stroke most profitable to his fast wickets, and will have an inborn tendency to back or front foot as circumstances demand.

Now the cricketer transplanted to alien conditions has to proceed largely by conscious calculation until such time as his instincts are attuned, and it was apparent that May's team were largely in this stage. Such being so, it was inevitable that the home side made much greater and better use of their resources, but in doing so did much to accelerate this process of transition in their visitors. When the M.C.C. players became the England team in the next match it was apparent that the process was making satisfactory progress. Then the fielders were much more economically distributed, the bowlers found the best length more rapidly, and the batsmen had a surer idea of the pace and bounce of the ball from the pitch.

There was no exciting finish to the First Test Match which passed peacefully away, unresolved at the end of its allotted span. On a wicket reminiscent of the 'thirties at their most placid, 1116 runs were scored for the fall of 18 wickets. From this it will be gathered that the batsmen for the most part hogged the proceedings. England omitted Subba Row, Andrew and Greenhough and suffered a great loss in that an injury kept Statham out. It was thought that his pulled leg muscle was due to a fall in the late and slippery stages of the colony match.

England won the toss and the match started off with a tremendous cannonade from the West Indies' fast bowlers. Hall is the senior partner, a tall, magnificently built man who runs over thirty yards with a powerful thrusting stride. His action, if not quite the classic wheel, has a magnificent final sweep of arm and his pace is very great. His opposite number, Watson, also tall and well built, has the slinging action of the javelin thrower, and is suspect when he bowls his faster bouncer. The opening spell contained a very high percentage of bouncers and unpleasantly short pitched balls, which rose between thigh and shoulder.

Pullar and Cowdrey met this onslaught with skill and resolution and Barrington battled splendidly for 128, but six wickets fell for 309, by no means a safe position in Barbadian conditions. With memories of Australia fairly fresh the traveller understandably felt that the end was not far off, but in this he was most agreeably confounded.

Dexter, well supported by his partners, played a magnificent innings. Those who had doubts about his future on that Australian trip must all have recognised a great advance towards the realisation of his great talents. He dealt majestically with the fast bowlers, and seemed to have shed any hesitancy in dealing with such an elusive customer as Ramadhin. His 136 was top-score and represented a series of strokes of the thumping power of Wally Hammond. The net gain to his side was 179 for the last four wickets, and a fairly certain release from any threat of defeat.

The West Indies started their innings just after lunch on the third day (surely a statement which would have provoked a tug on W.G.'s beard), and immediately struck disaster. McMorris was run out off a no-ball, and one wicket was down for six. At 68 Hunte was caught behind and at 102 Trueman bowled Kanhai. This was just fine, but English satisfaction steadily receded when no wicket fell for a most unconscionable time. Sobers, missed twice, made no third mistake, while the "veteran" Worrell flowed as imperturbably as Ol' Man River throughout Saturday, so that after a comfortable day's stay 165 runs had brought the total to 279.

On Monday the fourth wicket carried the score to 501 and it seemed that the West Indies, by forceful tactics after the scores had levelled, might at least have given England a fright. As it was Worrell batted with the most unaccountable caution so that when Alexander declared the match was as dead as a stonewaller's bat. The England opening pair once again made a capital impression, but it was largely in the nature of an academic exercise.

The bowlers, having little prospect, stuck to the job, and Trueman received some return for his unstinting efforts. The spinners spun to little purpose. Admittedly there were from time to time some interesting personal performances but the sort of match, wherein the first innings is completed at tea-time on the fifth day, just is not my sort of cricket.

The stay in Barbados had been most pleasant, and it was great fun to see John Goddard, Gerry Gomez and a lot of other old friends once more.

164

BARBADOS

Test No. 487—West Indies v England (Barbados) 1959-60

ENGLAND

G. Pullar	run out	65	not out ... 46
M. C. Cowdrey	c Sobers b Watson	30	not out ... 16
K. F. Barrington	c Alexander b Rama-dhin	128	
P. B. H. May	c Alexander b Hall	1	
M. J. K. Smith	c Alexander b Scarlett	39	
E. R. Dexter	not out	136	
R. Illingworth	b Ramadhin	5	
R. Swetman	c Alexander b Worrell	45	
F. S. Trueman	c Alexander b Rama-dhin	3	
D. Allen	lbw b Watson	10	
A. E. Moss	b Watson	4	
Extras	(B 4, LB 6, NB 6)	16	(B 7, LB 1, W 1) ... 9
Total		482	(o wkt) ... 71

WEST INDIES

C. C. Hunte	c Swetman b Barring-ton	42
E. McMorris	run out	0
R. Kanhai	b Trueman	40
G. Sobers	b Trueman	226
F. M. Worrell	not out	197
B. F. Butcher	c Trueman b Dexter	13
W. Hall	lbw b Trueman	14
F. C. M. Alexander	c Smith b Trueman	3
R. Scarlett	lbw b Dexter	7
C. Watson	} did not bat	
K. T. Ramadhin	}	
Extras	(B 8, LB 7, W 1, NB 5)	21
Total	(8 wkts dec)	563

WEST INDIES	O	M	R	W	O	M	R	W
Hall	40	9	98	1	6	2	9	0
Watson	32·4	6	121	3	8	1	9	0
Worrell	15	2	39	1				
Ramadhin	54	22	109	3	7	2	11	0
Scarlett	26	9	46	1	10	4	12	0
Sobers	21	3	53	0				
Hunte					7	2	9	0
Kanhai					4	3	2	0

ENGLAND	O	M	R	W
Trueman	47	15	93	4
Moss	47	14	116	0
Dexter	37·4	11	85	2
Illingworth	47	9	106	0
Allen	43	12	82	0
Barrington	18	3	60	1

FALL OF WICKETS

	Eng. 1st.	W.I. 1st.	Eng. 2nd.
1st.	50	6	—
2nd.	153	68	—
3rd.	162	102	—
4th.	251	501	—
5th.	291	521	—
6th.	303	544	—
7th.	426	556	—
8th.	439	563	—
9th.	478	—	—
10th.	482	—	—

Trinidad

THE QUEENS PARK IS THE LEADING CRICKET club in Trinidad and it is upon their ground that the main colony and Test Matches are played. The club celebrated its centenary in 1956 and has occupied its present site for over sixty years.

It is a very beautiful ground, indeed one of the most beautiful I have seen, comparing with Capetown or Adelaide. It sits in a bowl of picturesque hills, immediately surrounded by exotic trees and foliage, against which it matches a vivid green. Until comparatively recently the wicket was matting, but it is now a perfect surface of turf. That is perhaps hardly accurate for, as elsewhere in the West Indies, precious little grass is to be found on the actual wicket. This is made on a foundation of a special clay supplied by a sugar estate, who have the only source of supply on the island. It is rather akin to the bulli or Merri Creek soils of Australia, and is similarly laid on the table to a depth of about eighteen inches. It rolls out to a flawless shining surface of considerable durability, but again of small assistance to the struggling bowler. Despite a promise of great pace it was in fact not as fast as the Barbados pitch when put to the test.

Trinidad also has a tremendous cricket tradition. It has produced two unique if rather different figures in the cricket world, in the persons of Sir Pelham Warner and Learie Constantine, now a Minister in the Trinidadian Government. George John was a fine fast bowler who came to England in 1923, and whose son wrote the successful play, "Moon on a Rainbow Shore". In more recent times both Gerry Gomez and Jeff Stollmeyer captained the West Indies and have graduated to the Selection Committee. Incidentally, one of the lighter entertainments at Port of Spain used to be Gerry's fervent but eccentric admirer who would stand forth in front of the crowd to voice the thunderous and rhetorical question, "Who is the greatest all-round cricketer in the world?" and lead the tumultuous response, "Gerry Gomez!"

May's side were due to play three matches, two as M.C.C. against the Colony followed by the Second Test Match. The first Colony match at Port of Spain turned out to be quite an exciting affair after an unpromising start. The home side declared at 325 for 9 and the M.C.C. allowed a good off spinner named Corbie, and a good slow left hander, Singh, to run through them on a perfect wicket. A reasonable declaration left M.C.C. 262 to make in 210 minutes. Subba Row, Smith and Dexter this time sailed into the erstwhile successful bowlers and, finding them naked and unarmed, polished off the match with ten minutes to spare.

The second match was played at Pointe-à-Pierre at the other side of the island and was something of a fiasco. Ramadhin did not play in either match, and a weak side and turning wicket combined to end the match on the third day of the scheduled four. Personally, I was not unduly dismayed for I was enjoying myself staying on a sugar estate, where I was allowed to ride on the footplate of one of the few remaining steam locomotives.

When the sides of the Second Test Match were announced there was but one change in each, Singh replacing the gigantic off-spinning Scarlett and Statham, now recovered, coming in for Moss. The wicket looked the best yet, and the weather was pleasant when May again won the toss.

The opening barrage was more severe than ever, but Pullar and Cowdrey once again coped very competently, and all might have been well if Pullar had not played rather inside a ball on the leg side from Watson and been caught at the wicket, just at that point when a change of bowling must have been imminent. This taste of blood seemed to excite the bowlers for, from this moment until lunch time, the batsmen were attacked with a severity beyond anything in my experience. Bouncers flew high and frequent, and both bowlers bowled consistently short of a length so that the ball skidded breast high. Barrington being short of stature was at a great disadvantage but Cowdrey, determined not to sacrifice his wicket, took a good deal of punishment. At length Cowdrey, much harassed, carved at a ball outside the off stump and played on to such effect that both middle and leg stumps were knocked down. May got an equally warm reception and was out to a catch in the slips off another fast short ball following a roaring bouncer. With three out for 57 England were in a parlous state when lunch time came.

Watching this most hostile onslaught one had the curious feeling that it was delivered without evil intent, but with immense exuberance and little realisation of its dangers and implications. It was also a sad reflection that when the bowler is shorn of all his more graceful weapons the bouncer remains the one effective line of attack to those who have the pace to utilise it.

The afternoon brought a splendid recovery. Although frequently nonplussed, Barrington stuck grimly to the job, and Dexter played the fast bowlers with all the assurance of his commanding height and power of stroke. By the close of play the situation was again transformed with the score at 220 for four, a great deal better position than had at one time seemed possible.

Next day there were again sporadic outbursts of bouncing and bumping but, as is the accepted custom, the later batsmen were not threatened. Smith played calmly and resolutely and England totalled 382, a very much greater score than had at one time seemed possible.

When the West Indies continued their innings on Saturday morning they met with nothing but woe in the face of some splendid bowling by Trueman and Statham. It is but fair to say that England's strenuous efforts were attended by a fine run of fortune. Hunte played a ball on to his boot whence it shot up to short fine leg. Kanhai was LBW to a full toss. Sobers slashed at his third ball from Trueman and sent it bullet-like to May at third slip who got an outstretched hand to it, and popped it gently to Barrington at first. Solomon was run out quite unnecessarily, and Worrell, apparently upset by this, fell a victim once more to his old enemy Statham. Lunch time was 45 for five, and the West Indian defences burst right open. Statham, bowling magnificently with the old ball, had beaten Butcher about eight times in a couple of overs so hopes of another wicket were high and were soon realised after the interval.

The afternoon then saw some stiffer resistance but at 98 the eighth wicket fell when Singh was run out. The decision, a very proper one, was given by Lee Kow, a most competent local umpire; but it was the signal for uproar and chaos.

A dense section of the crowd packed together on a mound to the right of the pavilion had been evincing increasing signs of impatience and hostility whilst the day's disasters mounted. As Singh walked back the pent-up pressure of rum, congestion and frustration burst. A single bottle sailed in a silvery parabola on to the field and in a moment it was followed by a glacial barrage. The throwers could take no further action, being caged in by a stout wire grid, but from the opposite side of the ground a few spectators rushed on and this, as the case of the bottles, quickly became a flood. Very soon the players and umpires were surrounded, but the most turbulent of the invaders made it clear that they intended no harm towards the team. The umpires must have felt a lot less confident.

The Governor and Prime Minister were present and with Learie Constantine tried to appeal for order but were disregarded. At least, Learie made a good attempt to catch a bottle heaved in his direction, if not specifically intended for him. The team left the field and there was nought now to be done but to fetch the Riot Squad and the Fire Brigade.

When these arrived order was gradually restored after some pantomine with the hose which initially back-fired and drenched the counter-marksmen. Several arrests were made and the majority of peaceable citizens left the ground for it was clear there could be no further play, if for no other reason than that the outfield was carpeted with broken glass.

The ensuing situation was most admirably handled by Walter Robins and Peter May, but the blow to the feelings of good Trinidadians was bitter beyond alleviation. Many, amongst them old players, were in tears and felt the behaviour of the hooligan minority was a blot on the good name of the Colony which nothing could eradicate. However, by good management and the diplomatic bearing of the team the match started to time on Monday, indeed half an hour early to make up the loss. It was noticeable that the police were strongly reinforced but, in any case, the crowd was a great deal less, and one had the impression of a somewhat penitent atmosphere.

The remaining West Indies batsmen were soon disposed of and, with a lead of 270, May took the expected decision and batted again for, on these covered wickets, the only help a bowler can expect is from wear and tear. A fairly hustling second innings of 230 set the West Indies 501 to get in ten hours, a distant but not impossible target. But despite a fair start which saw 150 up with only Hunte and Solomon out it never looked to be a task within their grasp and, in the face of some further good bowling by Statham and Trueman, supported by Allen, the innings cracked and England won by 256 runs. Kanhai was alone in the glory of a very good century.

England were one up, a strong position as the result of a fine combined performance. All the batsmen had contributed to a great recovery from a position which a year before would have been irretrievable. The bowlers had been admirably led by the quicks and, if the tide flowed for them in the first innings, they certainly deserved their good fortune.

Test No. 488—West Indies v England (Trinidad) 1959-60

ENGLAND

Batsman	1st innings	R	2nd innings	R
G. Pullar	c Alexander b Watson	17	c Worrell b Ramadhin	28
M. C. Cowdrey	b Hall	18	c Alexander b Watson	5
K. F. Barrington	c Alexander b Hall	121	c Alexander b Hall	49
P. B. H. May	c Kanhai b Watson	0	c & b Singh	28
E. R. Dexter	c & b Singh	77	b Hall	0
M. J. K. Smith	c Worrell b Ramadhin	108	lbw b Watson	12
R. Illingworth	b Ramadhin	10	b Hall	41
R. Swetman	lbw b Watson	7	c Alexander b Watson	0
F. S. Trueman	lbw b Ramadhin	8	c Alexander b Hall	37
D. Allen	not out	4	not out	16
J. B. Statham	b Worrell	0	not out	0
Extras	(LB 3, W 1, NB 8)	12	(B 6, LB 2, W 4, NB 2)	14
Total		**382**	**(9 wkts dec)**	**230**

WEST INDIES

Batsman	1st innings	R	2nd innings	R
C. C. Hunte	c Trueman b Statham	8	c Swetman b Allen	47
J. Solomon	run out	23	c Swetman b Allen	9
R. Kanhai	lbw b Trueman	5	c Smith b Dexter	110
G. Sobers	c Barrington b Trueman	0	lbw b Trueman	31
F. M. Worrell	c Swetman b Trueman	0	lbw b Dexter	9
B. F. Butcher	lbw b Statham	9	c Trueman b Allen	7
F. C. M. Alexander	lbw b Trueman	28	c & b Barrington	0
K. T. Ramadhin	b Trueman		not out	11
Singh	run out		c Allen b Barrington	0
W. Hall	b Statham		b Statham	0
C. Watson	not out		run out	0
Extras	(LB 2, W 1)	3	(B 11, LB 6, W 2, NB 1)	20
Total		**112**		**244**

Bowling

W. INDIES

	O	M	R	W	O	M	R	W
Hall	33	9	92	2	11	5	35	5
Watson	31	5	100	3	9	2	42	3
Worrell	11·5	6	23	1	12	5	27	0
Singh	23	6	59	1	8	3	28	2
Ramadhin	35	12	61	3	28	8	54	1

ENGLAND

	O	M	R	W	O	M	R	W
Trueman	21	11	35	5	19	9	44	1
Statham	19·3	8	42	3	25	12	44	2
Allen	5	0	9	0	31	13	57	3
Barrington	16	10	15	0	25·5	13	34	2
Illingworth	7	3	8	0	28	14	38	0
Dexter					6	3	7	2

FALL OF WICKETS

	Eng. 1st	W.I. 1st	Eng. 2nd	W.I. 2nd
1st.	37	22	18	29
2nd.	42	31	79	107
3rd.	57	31	97	107
4th.	199	45	101	159
5th.	276	45	122	188
6th.	307	73	133	222
7th.	308	94	133	222
8th.	343	98	201	244
9th.	378	103	230	244
10th.	382	112	—	244

Jamaica

JAMAICA IS THE LARGEST OF THE BRITISH West Indian islands but its cricket history is shorter than the other main centres. Nonetheless the game flourishes there as happily as elsewhere in the islands and, to the visiting eye, the Jamaican crowd is at least as enthusiastic as any in the West Indies or, indeed, in the world. The island's proudest cricket boast to date is that it is the birthplace of George Headley, known in his time as " The Black Bradman ", and maybe the best batsman the West Indies have yet produced, despite much high grade competition.

The chief ground is Sabina Park which if less picturesque than Port of Spain is a very fine cricket pitch. The wicket is again one of great perfection and the natural good light is aided by large areas of white wall behind the bowler's arm at each end. These could with advantage to the visitor be painted a gentle shade of green, for the glare must be fairly trying in the early stages of an innings. The accommodation is on the whole very good, with the exception of the press box, which is the worst I have ever experienced on a Test Match ground.

The Colony Match was played on the neighbouring Melbourne Park ground and was a very dull affair, in which McMorris re-established himself as a starter for the West Indian side with a patient century.

The Test Match was a very different affair. Few international matches can have fluctuated so violently and so frequently and, while the whole six days was a period of tension, the hourly changes of fortune occurred right up until the closing overs.

The West Indies, who had included Nurse, Scarlett and McMorris for Worrell (with a bad ankle), Singh and Butcher, once again lost the toss and found themselves in the field, but made a very telling start. Another artillery battle with the fast bowlers saw Pullar, Barrington and May out with the score in the sixties. The pattern was now a familiar one. The opening batsmen set off quite comfortably and had all but seen the first assault off when Pullar was caught in the slips. This was the signal for another terrific burst of speed, especially from Hall, and the bouncer and short-ball flew from the pitch, freshened by the moisture of recent rains. May was caught at short leg off a bouncer but, after lunch, Cowdrey and Dexter put up a strong resistance. When the latter was caught behind Smith came in and was utterly shattered by a fast yorker, so that half the side were out for 113. Illingworth lasted by determined play until the last over of the day when he too fell to Alexander off the all-conquering Hall, so that was 165 for six.

The day had been largely a duel between Hall, who had bowled magnificently if one on occasions disagreed with his tactics, and Cowdrey who, although black and blue, had refused to budge and carried the innings. It was not a very encouraging picture from the English point of view.

Next morning was more cheerful. Cowdrey completed his splendid hundred and Allen played like a real Test Match batsman. The total of 277 was not exactly imposing but more than was to be expected at several earlier stages.

The West Indies innings was founded on a prolonged stand between McMorris and Sobers, whose styles were admirably contrasted, the solid right hander and the dashing left. The English fast bowlers certainly bowled more bouncers than they had done hitherto, as this was now the order of the day, but it was somewhat ironical that it was Statham, the best conducted on either side, who inflicted the first injury of serious consequence. A shortish ball hit McMorris in the ribs and, almost at once, he coughed up some blood. He made a courageous attempt to continue but was persuaded to retire, at which Nurse came in and went after the bowling right away. By the close the score was 291 for two, Sobers over his hundred and Nurse high on the wing.

The Saturday morning was one of golden opportunity for the West Indies; but they so misplayed their hand that by the end of the day an impregnable position had been frittered away and the game was again wide open. The West Indies had started the morning 14 runs on with eight wickets in hand, lost them all and, having taken none, were just 11 runs on when all was said and done.

Sobers went early LBW to Trueman, then Nurse and Solomon allowed themselves to be so pinned down that no more than 38 runs were added by the lunch interval. The attempt to rectify this error was altogether too precipitate. Solomon was out first ball, caught at the wicket off a slashing cut. Nurse tried to hit a good length ball from the off to the on and skied it. The innings then disintegrated and ended at 353. By the close Cowdrey and Pullar had played safely and well for 65 runs so the morrow started with some advantage to England, as the wicket was beginning to show some signs of age.

Cowdrey, who had been the quieter partner on the previous evening, burst forth in all his glory next morning and runs came apace. He drove and thumped the over-pitched ball with an effortless weight, and produced some fine hooks off the fast bowlers. He later said he had changed his guard to middle and off to be up to the line for the hook, and it certainly seemed to be sound policy.

Both openers went at 177, Cowdrey when three runs short of his second century. It was a great pity that he did not, in fact, join Russell, Hammond, Paynter, Sutcliffe and Compton, but nothing could detract from the grandeur of this performance.

After that things did not go so very well. The ball started to keep low and Dexter was out to an almost dead shooter from Watson. The reason for these creepers was in all probability the network of deep wide cracks which were now interlaced over the face of the wicket. When the ball pitched fair and square in such a crevice it failed to rise and Watson bowled quite a number which squatted.

May batted very well if his efforts seemed rather more laboured than his normal easy gait. He was eventually bowled by a vicious ball which moved away to hit the off stump and break the middle. I had the strong impression that he was in fact seeking a run to keep the strike and protect the lesser striker at the other end. At the close nine wickets were down for 280, which meant that 205 were needed for victory, a reasonable target, if not greatly increased in terms of runs and time. Much depended on the first few overs of Tuesday morning.

It was to be expected that the morning would start in a tremendous atmosphere of tension and excitement. As I have said, an immense amount depended on the last wicket, chiefly in terms of time, but a few extra runs would also affect the balance disproportionately in England's favour. In the event Allen and Statham batted like an opening pair, with the result that forty-five minutes were subtracted from the West Indies maximum time and 25 runs were added to an already exacting task. When, at twelve forty-five, Statham was LBW to Ramadhin's faster ball the position was that the last innings had less than four hours' actual play to make 230 runs to win. Although the somewhat changeable pitch seemed rather more reliable during the morning it may have been due to the ball failing to drop in the formidable cracks. This could of course be a matter of good fortune, and would not alter the fact that it could be a very difficult surface on which to maintain the necessary rate of a run a minute.

The last two batsmen had done all required of them. Allen again looked an excellent cricketer and must have earned the right to bat above Swetman and Trueman, a change which would materially extend the batting. Statham has always been a fine striker of the ball when required, but as a six day a week cricketer naturally economises in the matter of stamina.

As Hunte and McMorris started on their distant quest

Statham was once again in the picture. Having bowled a couple of balls with a slight limp he cut his run to four paces before leaving the field. Happily, it turned out to be his boot, not its contents, which was damaged, and it was readily repairable for his second over. England set a widely spaced field for the fast bowlers, having but one slip and a gully. This was a sensible arrangement on a wicket from which few snicks carried any distance, and while there was still a call to keep the scoring at a fairly low rate. At ten minutes to one Trueman produced a very good ball which moved away a shade from McMorris and struck his off stump about half way up. Eleven for one was a discouraging start for the home side but the batsmen pushed on so that the score was 30 for one by lunchtime and immediately on the resumption the batsmen went into the attack again. This was obviously their best line and runs started to come quick enough to cause May considerable anxiety. At 48 Trueman produced an almost identical ball to the destroyer of McMorris and Hunte's off-stump went down. Hunte had been most dangerous, getting 40 out of 48 but he was replaced by an equal menace in the shape of Sobers, and the chase was immediately resumed. First ball Sobers snicked where third slip would have stood, but the ball sailed safely away for four. The score kept pace with the clock under this pressure and, although the ball beat the bat occasionally, the batsmen looked safe enough against both spin and seam. Illingworth and Allen got a little turn, but the hoped for shooter was conspicuous by its absence.

A completely different hazard put an end to the partnership when Kanhai hit the ball to cover, started and stopped, to find Sobers half way down the pitch. Three were out for 86, but there was still time and batting in hand. Nurse swung and carved according to plan, but Trueman came back and produced the three-card trick in that he produced the same ball for the third time running to flatten Nurse's off-stump. Scarlett saw the score to 140 before he was LBW to Statham and Alexander came in for the last decisive burst. For the first over or two it looked as though the batsmen were still on the pursuit but, when the score had reached around 150 and there was still 80 to get in well under the hour, it was apparent that they had relaxed their efforts and would perforce settle for the draw.

At this point Kanhai went lame and presently a runner appeared, all ready and padded up, but Alexander waved him back. There was then some consultation between the captains which seemingly proved abortive for the game continued for a few minutes. Alexander then again approached May and it was apparent that he was, erroneously, asking if Kanhai could have the services of a runner, and equally obvious that May refused. A great demonstration arose at this and as Alexander consulted the umpires, which he should have done in the first place, tempers rose rapidly in all parts of the ground. The umpires apparently considered that a runner was not justified for the game then continued with Kanhai limping between the wickets.

Perhaps it is most convenient to complete the description of the incident at this point from information gleaned from those concerned at a later date. Apparently May was under the impression that Kanhai was attacked by a passing bout of cramp and suggested that he should be given a salt pill, at least a sound and practical measure had his surmise been correct. At this Alexander consulted the umpires and Lee Kow knew the rule, which plainly states the batsman can have a runner if incapacitated in the course of the match without reference to the opposing captain. Apparently his colleague was doubtful if Kanhai was entitled to help in the circumstances and the appeal was refused.

There was great indignation in both camps chiefly directed against May as it was felt that, whatever the rights and wrongs of the situation, he had been guilty of a churlish gesture. That he had been guilty of an error of judgement on the spur of the moment is no doubt true but I myself had nothing but sympathy for him when there was time to reflect on the circumstances. It later came to light that he was pretty unwell at the time but, apart from that, he was a much harassed man who, at the end of six days of great strain and tension, had a good deal on his mind at that moment. A sudden and unexpected request gave little time for measured thought and it seemed to me that many people who became quite unnecessarily excited were inclined to see the matter in this perspective when they had time to review it with greater thoroughness.

It could be said that the issue had been decided and the hunt abandoned before this occurred and, when Kanhai was bowled by Trueman, the only possibility of a decision was another quick wicket, but despite every effort this did not occur and the match ended in another draw. To say it petered out would be quite wrong for despite the lack of a final decision it was, as I have tried to indicate, a most eventful match right up to the closing overs.

We left Jamaica the following day and flew to the charming little island of Antigua, there to draw a healthy and pleasant breath before setting off for British Guiana.

ENGLAND

Batsman	First innings	R	Second innings	R
G. Pullar	c Sobers b Hall	66		
M. C. Cowdrey	c Scarlett b Ramadhin	114	c Alexander b Scarlett	97
K. F. Barrington	c Alexander b Watson	16	lbw b Solomon	4
P. B. H. May	c Hunte b Hall	9	c Alexander b Hall	45
E. R. Dexter	c Alexander b Hall	25	b Watson	16
M. J. K. Smith	b Hall	0	lbw b Watson	10
R. Illingworth	c Alexander b Hall	17	b Ramadhin	6
R. Swetman	b Hall	0	lbw b Watson	5
F. S. Trueman	c Solomon b Ramadhin	4		
D. Allen	not out	17	not out	12
J. B. Statham	b Hall	13	lbw b Ramadhin	23
Extras	(LB 4, W 10, NB 3)	17	(B 8, LB 10, W 3, NB 2)	23
Total		**277**		**305**

WEST INDIES

Batsman	First innings	R	Second innings	R
C. C. Hunte	c Illingworth b Statham	7	b Trueman	40
E. McMorris	b Barrington	73	b Trueman	1
R. Kanhai	run out	147	b Trueman	57
G. Sobers	lbw b Trueman	70	b Trueman	19
S. Nurse	c Smith b Illingworth	8	run out	11
J. Solomon	c Swetman b Illingworth		b Trueman	10
R. Scarlett	c Statham b Illingworth		not out	
F. C. M. Alexander	b Trueman	6	not out	12
K. T. Ramadhin	b Statham	0		7
W. Watson	not out	5		
W. Hall		0		
Extras	(B 6, LB 7, W 1, NB 2)	16	(B 9, LB 3, W 6)	18
Total		**353**	**(6 wkts)**	**175**

Bowling

W. INDIES

	O	M	R	W	O	M	R	W
Hall	31·2	8	69	7	26	5	93	1
Watson	29	7	74	1	27	8	62	4
Ramadhin	28	3	78	2	28·3	14	38	3
Scarlett	10	4	13	0	8	2	18	0
Sobers	2	0	14	0	8	2	12	0
Solomon	4	1	12	0	6	1	20	1

ENGLAND

	O	M	R	W	O	M	R	W
Statham	32·1	8	76	3	18	6	45	1
Trueman	29	10	82	2	18	4	54	4
Dexter	12	3	38	0				
Allen	28	10	57	1	9	4	19	0
Barrington	21	7	38	1	4	0	0	0
Illingworth	30	13	46	2	13	4	35	0
Cowdrey					1	0	4	0

FALL OF WICKETS

	Eng. 1st.	W.I. 1st.	Eng. 2nd.	W.I. 2nd.
1st.	28	12	177	11
2nd.	54	56	177	48
3rd.	68	299	190	86
4th.	113	329	211	111
5th.	113	329	329	140
6th.	165	329	258	152
7th.	170	341	269	—
8th.	215	347	269	—
9th.	245	350	280	—
10th.	277	353	305	—

Georgetown, British Guiana

GEORGETOWN, THE CAPITAL OF BRITISH Guiana, turned out to be the pleasantest town we saw in the Caribbean. The streets are wide and spacious, with pleasant tree lined walks down the centre where once had flowed canals. The older buildings are wholly constructed of wood, painted white and agreeably picturesque in surroundings of flowering shrubs. The general scene is unmistakably Dutch, for the colony was originally settled and developed by settlers from Holland. The weather during our stay was extremely good, the hot sun being tempered by the cool trade winds which blew gently but constantly.

The cricket ground of the Bourda club, the oldest in the Caribbean, is well laid out and good looking in itself but lacking in the superb mountainous background which makes Trinidad so outstandingly beautiful amongst cricket grounds. The wicket is again hard rather shiny clay, and one of the easiest in pace in the West Indies.

The most eagerly awaited feature of the Colony match was the bowling of Stayers who had at first been regarded as a likely rival to Hall and Watson. Apart from any other consideration, however, there had been a certain uneasiness about his action, and the selectors acted very properly in rejecting him when their own observations heightened these doubts. Otherwise one was rather wearily prepared for another slow, high scoring draw, and this the match proved to be.

There was another magnificent innings from Cowdrey which brought his aggregate for four innings to 459. When the home side, aided by a laborious century from Butcher, declared 375 for 6 wickets, he and Pullar put together 281 for the first wicket and M.C.C. went on to another outsize score.

Stayers made no great impression. In the ordinary process of bowling he had quite a nice wheeling action, but seemed to lack much whip at the finish. The result was that his pace was just quick and he tended to bowl full tosses from a flapping arm, rather than digging the ball down to a length. The bouncer was a very different pro- position. Without any visible warning he would suddenly snap the ball out like a shot from a gun and then the doubts about his action were plain to see. Pullar was caught standing by the first two bouncers he received, but once this menace was mastered there was little more danger and a lessening prospect of Stayers playing in the Test Match.

Soon after our arrival in British Guiana came the mel- ancholy news that May had for some time been suffering from the after effects of his operation. The wound was not properly healed and, in the heat and strain, he must have gone through much pain. At length he was forced to give up, which he did reluctantly; for, as I have said, he is not one to yield readily when his duty, as he sees it, to his side is concerned. At least he had the comfort of knowing that he had a most able man in Subba Row to take his place and, once the decision was made, could reflect that there is no place for a sick man in a week-long Test Match.

The major event in the West Indies preparations was the return of Walcott after a fairly long absence from their side. He had shown fine form in the Colony Match and was undoubtedly still a great material force apart from adding much to the general morale. With Worrell back in the side two thirds of the great trio were again in action. The snag facing the selectors was the injury to Ramadhin's shoulder and the discovery that Gibbs, his likeliest stand in, had a damaged finger. In the event Scarlett and Singh supplied the spin, with the addition of Sobers' "China- men."

Cowdrey took over the captaincy and followed in May's footsteps by winning the toss. Because of rain the start was delayed and only three overs were bowled before lunch; but these were sufficient to reveal that the wicket was as easy a pace as any seen so far. When Hall thrashed the ball down nearer to his own end it rose to an absurd height in a leisurely parabola to fall almost vertically into Alexander's hands.

The afternoon saw Cowdrey and Pullar once again run smoothly and competently into a sound first wicket stand. The fast bowlers in this instance looked ineffective but Singh, studied through field glasses, looked a very good proposition. He flighted the ball well from his loose easy action and spun it perceptibly, if the effect of this from the pitch was nil. Scarlett was steady, but Sobers was so erratic as to be disconcerting.

The score was 73 when Pullar was caught behind off Hall's first ball of a new spell, and Subba Row was given a hit ten minutes before tea. The second wicket soon took the running up again when Subba brought his solid powers of defence to bear, and it looked as though it would carry the day. But at 121 Subba Row tried to sweep the unpredictable Sobers to fine leg and was also caught at the wicket. Barrington was just in time to receive a most painful blow on the arm ducking a bouncer from Hall which didn't bounce and, in answer, hooked his assailant for a couple of fours, the day ending at 152 for two, a comfortable position but of no decisive advantage to either side.

The next morning was packed with action. Cowdrey pushed forward at Hall's third ball of the day and his fine innings ended with Alexander's third catch of the innings. With Dexter in, Barrington began to show signs of great distress, and soon retired clutching his injured arm. Smith pushed forward at a thunderbolt of good length from Hall and was clean bowled. Illingworth was out to a short ball from Sobers which he ill-advisedly tried to hit to square leg. Swetman was once again defeated by pace and LBW to Watson; with the result that England in a depressingly short time were 175 for 6.

However Dexter, playing finely, found solid support from Allen, a most useful and determined batsman. All went well until 219 when Dexter hooked Hall, and was caught by Hunte half-way back at square leg. Barrington reappeared to hold on until 250 and Trueman saw a bit more added. After that the last wicket added 27 most valuable runs so that the innings got to 295, a moderate enough score on this wicket.

Hall wound up with six for 90, another very fine performance. It was noticeable that when meeting with material success, as in his first spell of the day, he bowled a good length, with a very accurate control of direction and looked a beautiful fast bowler. He could produce at will the fast straight yorker or half-volley, which caused Smith and Swetman such difficulty, and the pity is that he is not under rigid instructions to bowl in this fashion at all times.

What struck one most forcibly about the West Indies tactics was the general lack of any air of urgency. Being one down they had to win, and should have been constantly on the attack. This they may have been, in a sense, for the results were good enough; but only 16 overs were bowled in the morning and there tended to be lengthy, and surely unnecessary, consultations between every over. The result was a somewhat leisurely atmosphere which must be psychologically wrong. A well trained side should not only be keyed up to the highest pitch when an opening is made but, like justice, this should be apparent. One has but to recall the Yorkshire side in its heyday, or an Australian team on the hunt, to realise the great moral force generated by every man being in his place and on his toes, straining to get at the batsman. Delays break the tension and dissipate the spirit of aggression so that the initiative can easily be lost. For cricket of all games is subject to violent changes in the attitudes and relative outlook of the contending parties.

When the West Indies batted McMorris and Hunte gave their side a good start by scoring 32 runs in the remaining 45 minutes, good going to Test Match standards. The next day was a very different story. Cowdrey displayed a real flair for the defensive arts of captaincy, placing his fields most skilfully, and using his bowlers with sound judgement. The bowlers implemented his plans very ably so that fast scoring was not easy. This did not, however, account for the fact that players of the calibre of the first four West Indians allowed themselves to be pinned down to no more than 107 runs in the day. The fact was that the West Indies, having established an early ascendancy in a match they were extremely keen to win, were unable to gauge the situation. No attempts were made to break up the field by playing for quick singles, and none to lift the ball over the close knit field, a most justifiable risk in the circumstances. The result was that, at the end of the third day, the West Indies had largely lost a good chance of forcing a win. In plain figures they had lost 32 minutes through rain but had scored only 107 runs off 68 overs bowled.

The next day was notable for a century from Sobers and a great spell of bowling by Trueman. Only 25 runs came in the first hour of Kanhai and Sobers, and their side fell further behind the clock.

After lunch Trueman had Kanhai caught off a slow full toss and there followed a splendid duel with Walcott. It ended at 212 when that great man, having made 9, was beaten by an in-dipping yorker which hit his leg stump. Worrell was much harassed for three overs, but survived and for the moment Trueman was spent. The batsmen went smoothly, but unhurriedly on to the close of play by which time they had scored 333.

Allen bowled Worrell second ball on Monday morning and six runs later had Sobers stumped off a very good ball which turned just enough. Cowdrey now had, as so many captains before him, to choose between the successful spinners and a new ball, immediately available. He chose the former course and, although a perfectly logical decision, it did not work out, and Alexander and Scarlett embarked on the first real attempt to push things along. They ran everything, saving the bat and by lunch time the West Indies had added 60 runs to make the total 392 for the loss of the two overnight batsmen. As these were Sobers and Worrell England could be well content.

184

Alexander was run out immediately after lunch and Singh hauled off his pads before the innings was declared at 402 for 8, a lead of 107 and a day and a half left for play. A West Indian win was now unlikely, unless England batted very poorly, especially as Watson was out of action with ligament trouble in an ankle.

Hall was ineffective so the burden fell on the spinners, who occasionally found a little turn. Cowdrey was stumped off a good leg-break from Singh at 40, but Pullar and Dexter played well until the last over of the day when Pullar was out playing back to Worrell, the ball being almost a shooter.

What flicker of life there was left in the match was extinguished by lunch time when no further wicket had fallen and the score was 163. Not one did fall in fact until 258, when Worrell made a magnificent catch at mid-off from a whistling drive by Dexter. The retiring batsman had made 110 in a style which will be fondly recalled fifty years hence as the elderly now think of Woolley and Spooner. If Subba Row was more rugged and less varied of stroke he also played a fine innings, getting well up to the line of the quick bowling, and keeping well on top of the spinners. The rest was a rather meaningless exhibition.

The Fourth Test Match was not a great game of cricket. There had been plenty of elegant batting on a perfect wicket by both sides, and some very good fast bowling by Hall and Trueman. The spinners again got little of a look in, and the most remarkable feature amongst them was the erratic bowling of the usually circumspect Sobers. For England Allen did much good work in uphill circumstances.

During the match came the dire news of Statham's anxieties. At the end of the match he flew home to succour his ailing young son and console his overwrought wife. He was a great loss and his departure could not but greatly affect the prospects for Trinidad.

Test 490—West Indies v England (Georgetown) 1959-60

ENGLAND

Batsman	1st innings		2nd innings	
G. Pullar	c Alexander b Hall	33	lbw b Worrell	47
M. C. Cowdrey	c Alexander b Hall	65	st Alexander b Singh	27
R. Subba Row	c Alexander b Sobers	27	lbw b Worrell	100
K. F. Barrington	c Walcott b Sobers	27	c Walcott b Worrell	0
E. R. Dexter	c Hunte b Hall	39	c Worrell b Walcott	110
M. J. K. Smith	b Hall	0	c Scarlett b Sobers	23
R. Illingworth	b Sobers	4	c Kanhai b Worrell	9
R. Swetman	lbw b Watson	4	c Hall b Singh	3
D. Allen	c Alexander b Hall	55	not out	1
F. S. Trueman	b Hall	6		
J. B. Statham	not out	20		
Extras	(B 7, LB 2, NB 6)	15	(B 6, LB 4, NB 4)	14
Total		295	(8 wkts)	334

WEST INDIES

C. C. Hunte	c Trueman b Allen	39
E. McMorris	c Swetman b Statham	35
R. Kanhai	c Dexter b Trueman	55
G. Sobers	st Swetman b Allen	145
C. L. Walcott	b Trueman	9
F. M. Worrell	b Allen	38
F. C. M. Alexander	run out	33
R. Scarlett	not out	29
C. Singh	b Trueman	0
W. Hall	not out	1
C. Watson	did not bat	
Extras	(B 4, LB 12, NB 2)	18
Total	(8 wkts dec)	402

W. INDIES	O	M	R	W	O	M	R	W
Hall	30·2	8	90	6	18	1	79	0
Watson	20	2	56	1				
Worrell	16	9	22	0	31	12	49	4
Scarlett	22	11	24	0	38	13	63	0
Singh	12	4	29	0	41·2	22	49	2
Sobers	19	1	59	3	12	1	37	1
Walcott					9	0	43	1

ENGLAND	O	M	R	W
Trueman	40	6	116	3
Statham	36	8	79	1
Illingworth	43	11	72	0
Barrington	6	2	22	0
Allen	42	11	75	3
Dexter	5	0	20	0

FALL OF WICKETS

	Eng. 1st	W.I.	Eng. 2nd
1st.	73	67	4
2nd.	121	77	110
3rd.	152	192	258
4th.	161	212	320
5th.	169	333	322
6th.	175	338	322
7th.	219	393	331
8th.	258	398	334
9th.	268	—	—
10th.	295	—	—

FOR THE FINAL TEST MATCH BOTH SIDES made some alterations and additions to their sides. England had lost the invaluable services of Statham but were strengthened by the inclusion of Parks who succeeded Swetman. The West Indies put the emphasis on their pace attack by including Griffith, the Barbadian fast bowler.

The weather in Port of Spain had been exceptionally dry for the time of year, and this was reflected in the colour and texture of the wicket which might be said to have a matt finish rather than the usual gloss. Looking at it one got the impression that it was more likely to give a bit of turn in the later stages of the Match than its predecessors had done, and this was the opinion of those who knew the ground best.

Cowdrey won the toss for England for the fifth and last time in the series, and went forth with Pullar to open the proceedings. Hall bowled the first over but Griffith was preferred to Watson at the other end. The new fast bowler had a nice supple wheeling action rather like his namesake or Francis of a generation ago. His pace was not devastating but he got a lot of bounce when he dropped short, and appeared to bring the new ball into the batsman. When the score was 19 he had his first success when he bowled a bouncer at Pullar, who seemed to be late in picking up the flight of the ball, and was caught in the slips off his gloves. It was the last success his side had for a long time.

Cowdrey and Dexter completely dominated the day's play in their pleasantly contrasting styles. The captain took a certain amount of bumping and bruising from the fast bowlers but it was notable that, since he had batted on middle and off and shown a readiness to hook, the bowlers were less aggressive in his direction. He might have been caught in the slips early on, but it was a very difficult chance; otherwise he was unhampered by anything the West Indies could bring to bear. Dexter looked rangy in style and physique beside Cowdrey's stout build and unhurried weight of stroke, but he hit the ball with a crisp power that frequently left the field standing. When 191 runs had been added it seemed they would last the day, but Dexter tried to sweep Sobers and, getting a top edge, the ball bobbed up between mid-off and mid-on at which the bowler ran back and made a very good catch. Five runs later Sobers made a "chinaman" lift to hit Cowdrey on the thumb and this time the ball popped up in front of the batsman, at which Alexander shot forward and made a fine catch right on the ground.

Subba Row and Barrington were together for the last session and the remarkable Mr. Hall now girded up his ample loins and fairly let fly. Subba Row met this assault with resolute calm but Barrington, who had taken a fair pasting in the course of the series, was obviously much beset. He was hit on the hand early on and in the last over of the day, took a real crack on the same finger which finished him for the moment with one ball to go. It was surprising to see that this partnership had already added 41 runs.

Next day the innings produced two most satisfactory features. Barrington did the best possible thing by throwing the bat at everything from the word go and, aided by a good slice of luck, hit himself out of his troubles, whilst adding some very useful runs to the score. Parks's first appearance was immensely satisfactory for not only did he meet Hall confidently, despite doubts about his ability against really fast bowling, but he played Ramadhin better than anyone else in the match. Despite these efforts the English batting was a disappointment after the great start and 393 not a great total in the circumstances.

When the West Indies batted they too had their misfortunes. Hunte was hit on the head by a bouncer from Trueman and had to retire, and the unfortunate McMorris again run out, this time off Trueman's boot while backing up. Alexander came in at number 3, and batted out the evening.

Next day of play was Monday and forty minutes of it were lost at the start because of rain. More time was lost in the afternoon but even these losses did not seem to awaken the West Indies to the urgency of the situation. At the close of play only 150 runs were on the board and little attempt had been made to break the cordon of deep set English fields, when everything called for enterprise and calculated risk. The home side were one down, 243 runs behind and there were 15 hours' play to come, weather permitting.

Next day brought considerably more enterprise and it looked as if the West Indies might after all even things up. The turning point came when Worrell played on to Trueman, at 216, and soon afterwards Moss got Kanhai and Sobers out in one over at 227 and 230. It was a sudden and tremendous reward for the Middlesex man who, after a lean trip, had bowled well through this innings. The tail, headed by Hall, made something of a recovery, but this was the rock upon which the ship split. The one remaining sensation was caused when Dexter bowled a bouncer at Hall which caused him to sit down in an abrupt and bewildered consternation, and made the crowd laugh for five minutes. Half an hour before the close Alexander declared, and Hall ran up to bowl the first ball to Pullar. He reached the wicket and, having delivered the ball, from which Pullar took 3 to mid-off, was seen to have injured his side. The next ball was barely medium pace. The third was exactly similar and Cowdrey turned it gently and at convenient height to Worrell at short leg. All, especially bowler and striker, were greatly astonished at this but, one reflected, Cowdrey *had* to fail sometime, and anyway he had just heard that he was the father of a second bouncing boy. Allen came in and with Pullar saw the evening out.

Wednesday's cricket child was full of thrills with the match and the outcome of the series swinging to and fro almost in time to the town clock. Pullar and Allen went briskly to 69 when the junior member was run out after a very useful night watchman's innings. Pullar was caught and bowled just before lunch, and after it Sobers and Ramadhin began to get something out of the pitch and bowled very, very well. Ramadhin's box of tricks is well known if still occasionally baffling, but Sobers is a more recent problem. He bowls his left hand off-breaks and googlies something like Fleetwood-Smith in pace and method and, if less ferocious of spin, is equally hard to spot in intention. Like the old Aussie master he is erratic, but deadly on occasions. Against these two Dexter with a bit of luck (dropped at square leg at 30 and off a sitting return by Worrell at 32) played confidently, as did Subba Row; but there was a fine air of tension. At 136 Subba was LBW, and at 145 Dexter over-played his luck and ran himself out. Barrington fell to a short leg catch and this was 148 for six, and something pretty near defeat. Smith and Parks were now together and faced, not only with a major task, but a pretty problem in the tactics required to accomplish it. If a wicket fell the remaining batting on current form was negligible, and one mistake was therefore the end. Yet over caution might well lead just to this.

The batsmen found the right answer with the instinct of the true cricketer. They had a careful look and then played their respective natural games. The result was a grand bit of cricket. The spinners were defeated and the new ball cracked all about so joyously that 60 runs came off it in 45 minutes. True, Hall bowled but two very gentle overs, but Watson and Griffith were a formidable pair. This 45 minutes was fatal to West Indies' hopes and must have gone a good way to establishing Parks as a regular future member of the England side.

The last day was one of anti-climax for, when Cowdrey declared, it could only be a draw and the issue had been decided. There was much discussion as to when Cowdrey should declare. One school of thought was for making a gesture by a comparatively early closure and going for a win, while the other felt that having fought such a swaying battle so hard and long that to make sure was better than to make a gesture. The writer was certainly in favour of the latter.

Parks and Smith went off again at a brisk rate until half an hour before lunch when the rate of scoring fell so that by lunchtime they were 91 and 76 respectively with the total at 318 for 6. The only thing left in the match now was possibly some measure of light entertainment. Parks went on to complete his hundred but Smith fell to Hunte, hardly recognised as an international bowler, at 96 and the innings ended at 350 for 7.

The West Indies also made safe after which they supplied the desired light entertainment aided by the M.C.C.'s less recognised bowlers. Smith on being hit for a couple of sixes flew the white flag of surrender which gave everyone a much needed laugh, and the day ended quite happily.

It was a fair judgement that the better *team* had won, a point which was duly stressed in the West Indian Press. The series had been very evenly contested, and very few can have fluctuated for and against both parties to the extent that the play did in this case. It was here that a closely knit and easily manoeuvrable team were better able to seize their opportunities. The West Indies have abundance of talent, but it wants welding together and focus. Throughout the series it struck one that when they had achieved a commanding position they failed to realise the urgency of swift and concentrated exploitation. Alexander was a very good captain in many respects and certainly a keen one but, perhaps for many and complex reasons, he seemed to steer a rather unwieldy ship. This impression may have been exaggerated by the fact that the general level of the English fielding was much superior, which widened the disparity in team-work.

It will be interesting to see how the West Indians fare against the Australians next winter. Their progress will be of the utmost consequence to followers in England.

BOWLER'S TURN

Test No. 491—West Indies v England (Trinidad) 1959-60

ENGLAND

Batsman		1st		2nd
G. Pullar	c Sobers b Griffith	10	c & b Sobers	54
M. C. Cowdrey	c Alexander b Sobers	119	c Worrell b Hall	0
E. R. Dexter	c & b Sobers	47	run out	47
R. Subba Row	c Hunte b Hall	76	lbw b Ramadhin	13
K. F. Barrington	c Alexander b Ramadhin	22		
M. J. K. Smith	b Ramadhin	69	c McMorris b Sobers	6
J. M. Parks	c & b Sobers	20	c Alexander b Hunte	96
R. Illingworth	c Sobers b Ramadhin	43	not out	101
D. Allen	c sub b Ramadhin	0	run out	25
F. S. Trueman	not out	7	not out	2
A. E. Moss	b Watson	10		
Extras	(B 7, NB 9)	16	(B 2, LB 3, NB 1)	6
Total		393	(7 wkts dec)	350

WEST INDIES

Batsman		1st		2nd
C. C. Hunte	not out	72	st Parks b Illingworth	36
E. McMorris	run out	13	lbw b Moss	2
F. C. M. Alexander	b Allen	26	not out	4
G. L. Sobers	b Moss	92	not out	49
C. L. Walcott	st Parks b Allen	53	c Parks b Barrington	22
F. M. Worrell	b Trueman	15	c Trueman b Pullar	61
R. Kanhai	b Moss	6	c Trueman b Illingworth	34
K. T. Ramadhin	c Cowdrey b Dexter	13		
W. Hall	b Trueman	29		
C. Griffith	not out	5		
C. Watson	did not bat			
Extras	(B 6, LB 4, NB 4)	14	(LB 1)	1
Total	(8 wkts dec)	338	(5 wkts)	209

Bowling

W. INDIES	O	M	R	W		O	M	R	W
Hall	24	3	83	1		4	0	16	1
Griffith	15	2	62	1		9	1	40	0
Watson	18·2	3	52	1		14	1	52	0
Ramadhin	34	13	73	4		34	9	67	1
Worrell	8	1	29	0		22	6	44	0
Sobers	20	1	75	3		29	5	84	2
Walcott	4	2	3	0		7	2	24	0
Hunte						5	1	17	1

ENGLAND	O	M	R	W		O	M	R	W
Trueman	37·3	6	103	2		5	1	22	0
Moss	34	3	94	2		4	0	16	1
Allen	24	4	61	2		15	2	57	0
Illingworth	12	4	25	0		16	3	53	2
Dexter	4	1	20	1					
Barrington	8	0	21	0		8	2	27	1
Subba Row						1	0	15	0
Smith						1	0	11	0
Pullar						1	0	15	0
Cowdrey						1	0	15	0

FALL OF WICKETS

	Eng. 1st.	W.I. 1st.	Eng. 2nd.	W.I. 2nd.
1st.	19	26	3	11
2nd.	210	103	69	72
3rd.	215	190	102	75
4th.	268	216	136	107
5th.	317	227	145	194
6th.	350	230	148	
7th.	350	263	345	
8th.	374	328		
9th.	388			
10th.	393			

Note.—S. Nurse held the sub catch for West Indies.

TEST AVERAGES

TEST AVERAGES

ENGLAND—BATTING & FIELDING

	Tests	I.	N.O.	Runs	H.S.	Avge.	100	50	Ct.	St.
E. R. Dexter	5	9	1	526	136"	65·75	2	2	1	—
M. C. Cowdrey	5	10	1	491	119	54·55	2	2	1	—
K. F. Barrington	5	9	0	420	128	46·66	2	1	2	—
G. Pullar	5	10	1	385	66	42·77	—	3	1	—
R. Subba Row	2	4	0	162	100	40·50	1	1	—	—
M. J. K. Smith	5	9	0	308	108	34·22	1	1	3	—
D. Allen	5	9	4	171	55	34·20	—	1	—	—
P. B. H. May	3	5	0	83	45	16·60	—	—	1	—
J. B. Statham	3	4	1	46	20"	15·33	—	—	6	—
F. S. Trueman	5	8	2	86	37	14·33	—	—	6	—
R. Illingworth	5	8	1	92	41"	13·14	—	—	1	—
R. Swetman	4	7	0	58	45	8·28	—	—	6	1
A. E. Moss	2	2	0	5	4	2·50	—	—	—	—

Played in one Test: J. M. Parks 43 & 101" (1 ct. 2 st.).

ENGLAND—BOWLING

	Overs	Mdns.	Runs	Wkts.	Avge.	5wI.	10wM.
F. S. Trueman	220·3	62	549	21	26·14	1	—
J. B. Statham	130·4	42	286	10	28·60	—	—
E. R. Dexter	64·4	18	170	5	34·00	—	—
K. F. Barrington	106·5	41	217	5	43·40	—	—
D. Allen	197	53	417	9	46·33	—	—
A. E. Moss	85	17	226	3	75·33	—	—
R. Illingworth	196	61	383	4	95·75	—	—

Also bowled: M. C. Cowdrey 2-0-19-0, G. Pullar 1-0-1-1, M. J. K. Smith 1-0-15-0, R. Subba Row 1-0-2-0.

ENGLAND—CENTURIES

K. F. Barrington (2)—128 at Barbados, 121 at Trinidad.
M. C. Cowdrey (2)—114 at Kingston, 119 at Trinidad.
E. R. Dexter (2)—136" at Barbados, 110 at Georgetown.
J. M. Parks (1)—101" at Trinidad.
M. J. K. Smith (1)—108 at Trinidad.
R. Subba Row (1)—100 at Georgetown.

WEST INDIES—BATTING & FIELDING

	Tests	I.	N.O.	Runs	H.S.	Avge.	100	50	Ct.	St.
G. Sobers	5	8	1	709	226	101·28	3	1	7	—
F. M. Worrell	4	6	1	320	197"	64·00	1	1	4	—
C. C. Hunte	5	8	1	291	72"	41·57	—	3	1	—
R. Kanhai	5	8	0	325	110	40·62	1	2	2	—
C. L. Walcott	5	3	0	84	53	28·00	—	1	2	—
E. McMorris	4	6	0	124	73	20·66	—	1	1	—
F. C. M. Alexander	5	8	2	108	33	18·00	—	—	1	1
R. Scarlett	3	4	1	54	29"	18·00	—	—	2	—
K. J. Solomon	2	4	1	50	23	16·66	—	—	—	—
W. Hall	5	6	3	48	29	16·00	—	—	1	—
B. F. Butcher	2	3	0	31	13	10·33	—	—	—	—
K. T. Ramadhin	4	3	0	41	23	10·25	—	—	2	—
C. Singh	2	3	0	11	11	3·66	—	—	—	—
C. Watson	5	3	1	3	3	1·50	—	—	—	—

Played in one Test: S. Nurse 70 & 11. C. Griffith 5.

BOWLER'S TURN

WEST INDIES—BOWLING

	Overs	Mdns.	Runs	Wkts.	Avge.	5wI.	10wM.
K. T. Ramadhin	248.3	83	491	17	28.88	—	—
W. Hall	236.2	49	679	22	30.86	2	—
C. Singh	84.2	35	165	5	33.00	—	—
C. Watson	199	39	593	16	37.06	—	—
F. M. Worrell	115.5	37	233	6	38.83	—	—
G. Sobers	114	14	356	9	39.55	—	—
R. Scarlett	134	53	209	2	104.50	—	—

Also bowled: C. Griffith 24.3-102-1, C. C. Hunte 12-3-26-1, R. Kanhai 4-3-2-0, J. Solomon 17-2-51-1, C. L. Walcott 20-4-70-1.

WEST INDIES—CENTURIES

G. Sobers (3)—226 at Barbados, 147 at Kingston, 145 at Georgetown.
R. Kanhai (1)—110 at Trinidad.
F. M. Worrell (1)—197" at Barbados.

TEST SUMMARY

England scored 3119 runs off 1209 overs for the loss of 84 wickets—an average of 37.13 runs per wicket and a scoring rate of 42 runs per 100 balls received.

West Indies scored 2396 runs off 1005.4 overs for the loss of 65 wickets—an average of 36.86 runs per wicket and a scoring rate of 39 runs per 100 balls received.

TOUR AVERAGES—FIRST-CLASS MATCHES
BATTING & FIELDING

	M.	I.	N.O.	Runs	H.S.	Avge.	100	50	Ct.	St.
J. M. Parks	2	3	1	327	183	163.50	2	—	1	2
M. C. Cowdrey	11	18	2	1014	173	63.37	5	2	4	—
E. R. Dexter	12	18	2	908	136"	56.75	3	5	3	—
R. Subba Row	9	14	3	598	110	54.36	2	4	4	—
G. Pullar	11	18	2	777	141	48.56	1	5	1	—
K. F. Barrington	12	19	1	830	128	46.11	3	4	7	—
M. J. K. Smith	13	19	2	649	111	38.17	2	3	5	—
P. B. H. May	9	12	0	389	124	32.41	1	—	1	—
D. Allen	9	12	5	199	55	28.42	—	1	3	—
R. Illingworth	12	16	2	353	100	25.31	1	2	3	—
R. Swetman	9	12	1	177	45	16.09	—	—	9	2
J. B. Statham	6	8	3	78	20"	15.60	—	—	1	—
T. Greenhough	6	4	3	15	8"	15.00	—	—	1	—
F. S. Trueman	10	13	2	153	37	13.90	—	—	11	—
K. V. Andrew	4	1	0	4	4	4.00	—	—	7	5
A. E. Moss	8	5	1	15	5"	3.75	—	—	—	—

BOWLING

	Overs	Mdns.	Runs	Wkts.	Avge.	5wI.	10wM.
F. S. Trueman	342.3	86	883	37	23.86	2	—
D. Allen	305	94	639	23	27.78	1	—
T. Greenhough	182	43	590	21	28.09	1	—
J. B. Statham	213	57	493	15	32.86	—	—
K. F. Barrington	237.3	64	619	17	36.41	—	—
A. E. Moss	251	56	687	13	52.84	—	—
E. R. Dexter	192.4	36	637	11	57.90	—	—
R. Illingworth	365	107	781	11	79.00	—	—

Also bowled: M. C. Cowdrey 3-0-36-0, G. Pullar 1-0-1-1, M. J. K. Smith 2-0-22-0, R. Subba Row 53-7-169-4, R. Swetman 1-0-10-0.

CENTURIES

M. C. Cowdrey (5)—173 v Trinidad, 114 in 3rd Test at Kingston, 115 v Leeward Islands, 139 v British Guiana, 119 in 5th Test at Trinidad.

K. F. Barrington (3)—128 in 1st Test at Barbados, 121 in 2nd Test at Trinidad, 103 v Berbice.

E. R. Dexter (3)—136" in 1st Test at Barbados, 107 v Leeward Islands, 110 in 4th Test at Georgetown.

J. M. Parks (2)—183 v Berbice, 101" in 5th Test at Trinidad.

M. J. K. Smith (2)—108 in 2nd Test at Trinidad, 111 v Jamaica.

R. Subba Row (2)—110 v Leeward Islands, 100 in 4th Test at Georgetown.

R. Illingworth (1)—100 v Berbice.

P. B. H. May (1)—124 v Jamaica.

G. Pullar (1)—141 v British Guiana.

BOWLERS TAKING FIVE WICKETS IN AN INNINGS

F. S. Trueman (2)—5-22 v Windward Island, 5-35 in 2nd Test at Trinidad.

D. Allen (1)—7-33 v Trinidad.

T. Greenhough (1)—6-32 v Windward Islands.

THE PAVILION LIBRARY

All books from the Pavilion Cricket Library are available from your local bookshop, price £12.95 hardback, £5.95 paperback, or they can be ordered direct from Pavilion Books Limited.

In Celebration of Cricket
Kenneth Gregory

The Best Loved Game
Geoffrey Moorhouse

Bowler's Turn
Ian Peebles

Lord's 1787–1945
Sir Pelham Warner

Lord's 1946–1970
Diana Rait Kerr and Ian Peebles

P. G. H. Fender
Richard Streeton

Through The Caribbean
Alan Ross

Hirst and Rhodes
A. A. Thomson

Two Summers at the Tests
John Arlott

Batter's Castle
Ian Peebles

The Ashes Crown the Year
Jack Fingleton

Life Worth Living
C. B. Fry

Cricket Crisis
Jack Fingleton

Brightly Fades The Don
Jack Fingleton

Cricket Country
Edmund Blunden

Odd Men In
A. A. Thomson

Crusoe on Cricket
R. C. Robertson-Glasgow

**Benny Green's
Cricket Archive**

Please enclose cheque or postal order for the cover price, plus postage:

UK: 65p for first book; 30p for each additional book to a maximum of £2.00

Overseas: £1.20 for first book; 45p for each additional book to a maximum of £3.00

Pavilion Books reserve the right to show new retail prices on covers which may differ from those previously advertised in the text or elsewhere and to increase postal rates in accordance with the Post Office's charges.